Torin King - Harpist - at Mt Wilson

SPELLING IT OUT - THE EDITORS RAVE
PROTECT THY SELF

Yes this issue is late. My deepest apologies. Since the start of the new year we have been battling a drought, then fires, then floods and now CORVID19. (Oh and my youngest son got married) But **Magick Magazine** has made it through and it is out for another issue! Yay!!!

Our beautiful magickal Harlequin cover model is Kaylee McKenzie, she is a solitary practitioner, from the sleepy rural Queensland town of Boonah, who loves all things Egyptian and she has Cystic Fibrosis. CF is a genetic disease that weakens the lungs and makes her very susceptible to diseases like CORVID19. She is in the high risk category that must self-isolate during the pandemic for her own protection. I am very proud for her to be my daughter-in-law (not married to the one mentioned above, she is the partner to my oldest son) so naturally when this craziness all started, I did the interfering mother-in-law thing and recommended ancient traditional therapies.(see below) I know that if she died it would break my son's heart, but it would break all of our hearts too. Not only is she beautiful and a talented fashion/graphic designer in her own right, she is also a really lovely caring soul who is almost as big a comic/DC/Marvel geek as me. We all love her.

HOW TO MAKE YOUR OWN CORVID19 PROTECTION KITS

If you are in a high risk category here are some traditional ways to help, strengthen your system & keep yourself safe from any viral infection

TUMERIC -The yellow herb! Contains a substance called curcuminoid. Won't kill a virus but stops it reproducing. Has been used as an anti-viral in the ancient Aryuda Veda tradition for approx. 2 millennia, & they haven't lost a patient to it yet!!! In fact India is the country with the 2nd highest population in the world yet has one of the lowest infection/death rates, even though it has poor health care. Tumeric is a part of very daily meal there. Tumeric must reach a saturation point in the system of chronic virus suffers. Fresh is best. Take about as much as your little finger nail 3 x per day. The power is fine too. No Seriously. It is a fine powder. Don't breath in as you place the teaspoon of it on your tongue before you swallow the water. Other wise an uncontrollable coughing fit will result in a yellow kitchen/bathroom. It is actually much easier to mix it into your food. Clinical studies have shown Turmeric Is the Best Anti-Viral for enveloped viruses, like the Corona due to the high amount of curcuminoid, preventing most viruses from invading new cells •A natural pain reliever & primary anti-inflammatory. •Promotes wound healing is antiseptic & analgesic can be applied topically •Clinical studies have shown turmeric has anti-asthmatic properties too • plus its good for lots of other good things.

QUININE -Quinine is a parasite medication used to treat malaria and babesiosis. It is made from the bark of cinchona tree. Clive Palmer has offered to fund a free oral vaccine for the Australian public made from this natural substance. It is also used to make India tonic water. If you drink tonic water please make sure that the tonic water is made from real quinine not just flavour. there is an easy way to tell. Tonic water, in becomes ultraviolet in "black light" as the quinine content of tonic water causes it to fluoresce under black light. The Quechuas of South America, would mix the ground bark of cinchona trees with sweetened water to offset the bark's bitter taste, thus producing something similar to tonic water to stop shivering.

WEAR EYE PROTECTION IN PUBLIC -Most viruses are communicated via expectorant landing in eyes. It is very rare that things will get into you mouth or nose unless you touch them with hands that have touched some fresh infectious material. Masks are to prevent expectorant leaving you. If you are infected you should wear them. However, for the healthy, it is a false feeling of security.

WASH YOUR HANDS Disposable glove & hand sanitiser. Witches have always been practitioners of the Pagan Practise of Hygiene. The pentagram was a symbol of Pythagoras's main deity Hygeia, patron goddess of hygiene. When they burnt the midwives who followed the Pagan practise of hygiene, as superstitious nonsense believers (how can anything that you can't see kill you?) we had The Black Plague. The medical profession was still struggling to accept infection from germs in the 1930s. Witches have practised hygiene since 500BC. Without a doubt, public hygiene is the number 1 thing to restrict a new plague.

Every Blessing to you - Shé

And if you are in a high risk category...

© Shé D'Montford 2020

Magick Magazine No. 9

TABLE OF CONTENTS

Our theme this issue is BEING SAFE & HEALED BY MAGICK.
So find out what The Magick Magazine uncovered to sooth you!

SPELLING IT OUT - THE EDITORS RAVE	2	THE WEEKLY SEER	43
TABLE OF CONTENTS	3	CASTING MAGICK BY POST	44
THE MAGICK OF HARLEQUIN	4	DIVINE FEMININE	46
AMANDA PALMER : DROWNING IN THE SOUND	6	NEPTUNE'S SCEPTRE	48
MAGICKAL STAR WATCH	7	THE WITCH'S ALMANAC	50
AMANDA'S NOT HERE TO F*CK SPIDERS	8	FUNNY PHOTOS	59
WEST COUNTRY SPELLS	10	ENHANCING RITUALS WITH CRYSTALS	60
JOHN SAFRAN VS THE OCCULT	11	LOVE INVOCATION	61
AYAHUASCA MEDICINE	12	CUDDLE THERAPY - 62	62
FELLOW TRAVELLERS FOR THE GODDESS	17	SEKHEM EGYPTIAN LIVING LIGHT	63
COUNCIL SPONSORS FAIRYTALES & FOLKLORE	18	HELP PAGANISM TO BECOME	
THE ISLAMIC GREENMAN	19	A RECOGNISED DENOMINATION IN AUSTRALIA	64
JOEY POTTER PAGAN 3D ARTIST	20	BOOKS BY SHÉ D'MONTFORD	65
HERMETIC INVOCATION TO APHRODITE GODDESS OF LOVE	22	THE WITCHES BALL 2019	66
PAMELA COLEMAN-SMITH	24	MAGICKAL CLASSIFIDES	68
ISRAEL REGARDIE INITIATION & PSYCHOTHERAPY	30	SYMBOLS & THEIR MEANINGS	69
THE ART OF IMRE ZSIDO	36	WAYS YOU CAN CONNECT WITH YOUR GUIDES	71
THE ESOTERIC GARDEN	38	ONLINE COURSE IN MAGICK	72

M A G I C K   1 0   I S B N   9 7 8 - 0 - 9 9 4 3 5 4 1 - 7 - 4

Disclaimer: By law, we need to add this statement. This book is for educational purposes only and does not claim to prevent or cure any disease. The advice and methods in this book should not be construed as financial, medical or psychological treatment. Please seek advice from a professional if you have serious financial, medical or psychological issues. By purchasing and reading this book, you understand that results are not guaranteed. In light of this, you understand that in the event that this book does not work or causes harm in any area of your life, you agree that you do not hold Shé D'Montford, Shambhallah Awareness Centre. Happy Medium Publishing, its employees or affiliates liable for any damages you may experience or incur. The primary reason for this publication is entertainment and education about Pagan practices. While Shambhallah Awareness Centre has used all reasonable endeavours to ensure the information in this book is as accurate as possible, it gives no warranty or guarantee that the material, information, or publications made accessible by them are not fit for any use whatsoever nor does that excuse you from using your common sense. Shambhallah Awareness Centre and Rev. Dr S. D'Montford accepts no liability or responsibility for any loss or damage whatsoever suffered as a result of direct or indirect use or application of any material, publication or information obtained from them. These images qualifies as fair use under copyright law as use rationale, used for critical commentary and discussion by a non-profit organisation. Any other uses of this image may be copyright infringement.

This magazine brought to you by Happy Medium Publishing a division of Shambhallah Awareness Center. This extract is based on information supplied by the Registrar of the Australian Business Register. Tax Concession status: THE SHAMBHALLAH CHURCH INC, a Charitable Fund, is endorsed to access the following tax concessions: Tax concession From GST Concession 01 Jul 2005., Income Tax Exemption 01 Jul 2000. Deductible Gift Recipient: THE SHAMBHALLAH CHURCH INC operates the following Funds, Authorities or Institutions. Gifts to these Funds, Authorities or Institutions may be deductible from 01 Jul 2000

Magick spelled with a "K," in the old Scottish fashion, indicates a number of belief systems that teach how to make changes in the external world according to your will. The "k" makes a distinction between deeply held beliefs & mere stage prestidigitation or trickery, as is indicated when spelled as "magic."

Proudly Australian owned, operated & produced. A not-for-profit publication. Contributed articles are not the personal opinions of this magazine or editors. Some content royalty free. Some content qualifies as fair use under copyright law as use rationale, this being some images & credited quotes, used for critical commentary & discussion of the topics by an educational non-profit organisation. Any other uses of this content may be copyright infringement. All other content © held by Shambhallah Awareness Centre, The Happy Medium Publishing Company & Shé D'Montford 2019 - However views expressed do not represent those of the publisher or associates.

Our Cover Photo Credits & Inside Cover - "The Magick of Harlequin" & detail inside cover
Model: Kaylee McKenzie https://m.facebook.com/kayleeelisemodel
Make-up: Bellaris Makeup Artistry
Photographer: Sabrina Audrey Photography https://m.facebook.com/Sabrina-Audrey-Photography-666317880470902/

THE HAPPY MEDIUM PUBLISHING COMPANY
THE MESSAGE IS IN THE MEDIUM

THE MAGICK OF HARLEQUIN

Magick Magazine No. 10

Before she was D.C. she was part of our Norse/Anglo-Saxon/Normand/English Pagan pantheon. Let's trace her history and how she evolved into a mass-media icon.

Harlequin, King of the Wild Hunt

Herla King (English: Herla cyning meaning "host-king") is a legendary king of the mythical Germanic Wild Hunt, accompanied by "the troop of Herlethingus" (familia Herlethingi). Chasing down evil souls and sending them to judgement in the afterlife. It is not a stretch to conclude that this is the original name from which the term Harlequin may have been derived. Herla, is often identified as Woden, or as a legendary king of the Britons, who became the leader of the Wild Hunt after a visit to the Otherworld, returning three hundred years later, after the Anglo-Saxon settlement of Britain. The story retells of Herla's encounter with an otherworldly being, his journey to the latter's homeland, his transformation into the leader of The Hunt after his return to the human realm, and, finally, the disappearance of Herla and his band during the first year of the reign of Henry II of England.

In the 9th century, the knight Hellequin of Boulogne, died routing the Normans, leading a pack of 'crazed devils' on a wild hunt through the English country side to get rid of them all. According to the legend that arose from this historic event, Hellequin and his band would fight at night with super-human power, taking the appearance of an army of ghosts. The name Harlequin was first used in the 11th century, in a French story that reverses the previous tale. In it a monk is pursued by a troop of demons when wandering on the coast of Normandy at night. These demons were led by a masked, club-wielding "familia herlequin."

Christian Passion Plays

Christian Passion Plays turned the fun of this character from European Pagan beliefs, into the fear of the devil. The first known appearance on stage of Harlequin, is dated to 1262, as the character of a masked and hooded devil in "Jeu da la Feuillière" (Leaf Game.) After this, Harlequin became a stock character in French passion plays. The later Harlequin's name, physical agility and trickster qualities, came, from this mischievous "devil" character in medieval passion plays. Harlequin was routinely paired with the character Clown or Joker, the mischievous and brutish foil for the more sophisticated, romantic, Harlequin. A fact that the writers for D.C. have explored in their comic universe. Dante Alighieri christianised this story further in the Cantos XXI and XXII from his "Dante's Inferno," of the 14th-century epic poem "Divine Comedy," by turning Harlequin into a devil by the name of Alichino (Italian for Harlequin).

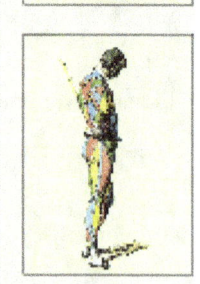

Commedia dell'Arte costumes from Maurice Sand's *Masques et Bouffons*, Paris 1860. Clockwise from above: Arlecchino, Arlequine, Arlequin, Colombine. © Witcard Publications

Harlequin in Commedia Dell'Arte

The character of Harlequin was popularised in Commedia dell'arte, the improvised theatre of 16th-century Italy. His or her clothes were covered in patches and face was covered with a half-mask. Through the centuries, Harlequin's costume became increasingly stylised, and the tatty patches became a regular diamond pattern. *The role of Harlequin in the plays, was that of a light-hearted, nimble, and astute magickal servant - part spirit - part human.* Harlequin often thwarted the evil plans of his master, and

pursued his/her own love interest. Sometimes unseen by the fellow stage characters, Harlequin moves invisible, bringing justice, or being the agent of change, often transforming his or herself into different people. Harlequin would transform the things surrounding him by hitting them with his magic bat or 'slapstick.' By hitting the backdrops and props with the bat, he/she would create scene changes. Wily and unscrupulous, Harlequin was always outrageously funny. An actor playing Harlequin had to be an acrobat as well as an actor.

Harley Quinn - in the garb of a more traditional Harlequin - with the Joker on the cover of *Batman: Harley Quinn* (Oct. 1999).
Art by Alex Ross/ DC Comics. Fair use rational

The characters from Commedia dell'arte, have become the archetypes we have become familiar with, in most sitcoms and many movies. As happens with many magickal archetypes, Harlequin overtly evolved into a comic book character, appearing in DC comes since the late 1940s. The character was re-created as Harley Quinn, by Paul Dini and Bruce Timm, and first appeared in Batman: The Animated Series in Sept 1992 & later in DC Comics' The Batman Adventures #12 (Sept 1993). Harley Quinn was an accomplice and lover of the Joker, whom she met while working as an intern psychologist at Gotham City's Arkham Asylum, where the Joker was a patient. She

Harley Quinn as she appears in the 5th volume of Suicide Squad-Aug 2017.
Her redesign brings her in line with Margot Robbie's portrayal of the character in the movie of the same name.
Art by Otto Schmidt/ DC Comics. Fair use rational

is now depicted as an anti-hero who left her abusive relationship with the Joker and her past as a super-villain behind. Harley Quinn has also been depicted as a recurring core member of the Suicide Squad. The character is also referred to by such epithets as the 'Cupid of Crime' and the 'Maiden of Mischief,' perfectly fitting the magickal character of her mythic origins.

It is wonderful to see popular media bringing this ancient Pagan deity back to the public and out into the light!

AMANDA PALMER : DROWNING IN THE SOUND

You worship the sun
And you're aching for change
But you keep starving your heart
You used to have sisters
You don't anymore
You worship the sun
But you keep feeding the dark...
SxSW

Two miles from town
I can't get out
I can't look down
If you can hear
If you're around
I'm over here
I'm over here
I'm watching everyone
I love Drowning in the sound

You worship the sun
But the moon's in the way
So get your armaments out
She's always looking for trouble
She's gonna get what's been coming to her
She's switching the tides
And we can't have that shit around
...And you're marching for peace
But you're lynching the bitch
That got up in your face
..And your body is a temple
And the temple is a prison
And the prison's overcrowded
And the inmates know it's flooding
And the body politic
Is getting sicker by the minute
And the media's not fake
It's just very Inconvenient...

Lyrics Extract from Drowning In The Sound on Amanda's new album: There Will Be No Intermission

31st October to 3rd November 2019

Earth Spirit-Natures Clothing & Giftware
Rear 200 Anson St - Orange - NSW - 2800

Ph. 02 6362 9773

http://earthspiritnatures.com.au
https://www.facebook.com/earthspiritshop

MAGICKAL STAR WATCH

I was called a whore and a WITCH says MADONNA

discussing the sexism, misogyny and bullying that women face. She spoke out about being raped on a rooftop with a "knife digging into my throat" when she first moved to New York but she would not let that act of hate define or limit her.. Madonna, the highest-grossing female artist of all time, resisted the notion that all was well and fair for women, particularly as they get older. Madonna takes pride in her ability to persevere in an industry that she said did not look kindly on older women artists and entertainers. "People say that I'm so controversial, but I think the most controversial thing that I've done is to stick around in the world of music, where 'To Age Is a Sin'. As you get older, you will be criticised, you will be vilified, and you will definitely not be played on the radio." Madonna has challenged sexual norms through her music, image and writing since the start of her career, pushing for "young women to be fully female and sexual, while still exercising total control over their lives. Women have been so oppressed for so long, they believe what men have to say about them, they believe they have to back a man to get the job done."Madonna warns against bowing to 'the rules of "the game"' — the established ideas that she said women are pushed to abide by. "You are allowed to be pretty and cute and sexy, but don't act too smart. Don't have an opinion. You are allowed to be objectified by men and dress like a slut, but don't own your sluttiness and do not — do not, I repeat — share your own sexual fantasies with the world." However, it is not just men who push these norms on women. Other women want you to play small and "to only be what women feel comfortable with you being around other men." Madonna would like women to be empowered and free from sexism, misogyny and bullying from everyone, men and women alike! - Yep! Sure talks like a true witch too! -

Madonna plays the sexy witch 'Elzpath' in a coven
(not the lead role)
in the quirky **Quentin Tarantino/Robert Rodriguez** collaboration
"The Four Rooms"
in the segment "The Missing Ingredient" written by Allison Anders

PAUL DEMPSEY
from
"Something For Kate"
was performing on an outdoor stage at a Perth as a support act for
DAVID BOWIE

on his final tour in 2004. Dempsey says :""The funny thing about it was it was so easy to forget you were talking to David Bowie because you were talking to a guy in jeans, a T-shirt and a baseball cap." The final down under show of Bowie's "Reality Tour" was ended by a large shooting star that blazed across the night sky. Many people at the concert let out a gasp of surprise. Dempsey turned to Bowie and asked how he had organised such a supernatural light show conclusion fo this act. To which Bowie replied:

"**Every man and every woman may be a star**
but Paul, if you work hard enough, one day you'll get a star all of your own."
It signalled the last live performance of this great magickian.
His final album released 8 years later was called:

BLACKSTAR

AMANDA'S NOT HERE TO F*CK SPIDERS

She is a Muse, Musician, Friend, Enemy, Teacher, Student, Mother, Daughter, Artist, Critic, Authentic, Fake, Activist, Pacifist, Divine, Human!

Amanda Palmer is a world-renowned singer, songwriter, activist, director, and blogger who first came to prominence as one half of the internationally acclaimed punk cabaret duo The Dresden Dolls. She is a fellow at the Berkman Institute for Internet & Society at Harvard University and has shown her underwear on Australian television. She currently avoids living in places including Boston, New York, and Melbourne with her husband, author Neil Gaiman, who is easily embarrassed. Palmer's TED Talk, "The Art of Asking," which she presented at a 2013 TED conference, has been viewed at least 8 million times around the world.

PAGAN FRIENDLY

Why would I write about a Catholic girl who is married to a wealthy Jewish man (Writer Neil Gaiman of American Gods; Sandman et al. fame) in a Pagan magazine?

Because, soooo many people in the Pagan community LOVE this woman. She is the strong, independent, outcast archetype, that represents the personal journey of so many Pagans. Yet, she has enough mainstream cred to be successful in her own right. She lives the unified life that is the ideal of every Pagan. She is connected to nature and to her fans as her family. She realises that all life is a reciprocal act of giving. So she bears her soul and her body. She lives in an Adam's Family style home. She is irreverent and spiritual ... oh and she makes great music too! Now, she is here in Australia.

AMANDA F*CK*NG PALMER-AMANDA ASKING PALMER-AMANDA GIVING PALMER-AMANDA GODDESS PALMER

Amanda Palmer's 'THERE WILL BE NO INTERMISSION' WORLD TOUR DOWN UNDER will be A NIGHT OF PIANO, PAIN & LAUGHTER. Palmer arrives on the cusp of a brand new decade to bring Woodford Folk Festival into 2020 over New Year's Eve before heading south to Launceston to tackle an intense and unprecedented residency at MONA in January. As an ambassador for Adelaide Fringe in 2020, she'll perform across two nights in Adelaide in February as well as headlining performances in Melbourne, Brisbane, Canberra, Sydney, Perth and Darwin throughout the summer. 'There Will Be No Intermission' is a seated theatre experience that features Palmer performing solo on grand piano and ukulele without a back-up band. The show is a night of graphic, honest and funny storytelling that Palmer claims is her *"most human and vulnerable stage-show to date"*. Palmer's show bares her soul, navigating through the raw and the hilarious.

Palmer's third solo LP has been entirely crowd-funded by over 15,000 patrons on Patreon, again! There Will Be No Intermission is the multi-faceted artist's most powerful and personal collection to date, with songs that tackle the big questions: life, death, grief and how we make sense of it all. Wonderful Pagan themes! This one-of-a-kind artist has miraculously moulded humour, tears, confession, and naked personal pain into a matchless piece of work that could very well have been morose and gloomy but is, instead, deeply relatable, healing and inspiring. While the themes may be dark, the album's overall sonic and lyrical mood is one of triumph in the face of life's most ineffably shitty circumstances. Of this time in her life Palmer says:

> "THE LAST SEVEN YEARS HAVE BEEN A RELENTLESS PARADE OF GRIEF, JOY, BIRTH AND DEATH, AND ALL OF IT HAS GALVANISED ME TO THE CORE: AS A WRITER, AS A WOMAN, AS AN ARTISTIC SERVANT,... I ALSO HAD NO IDEA THAT MY 15,000 PATRONS – WHO HELD MY HAND THROUGH THIS ENTIRE PROCESS – WOULD HAVE THE PROFOUND EFFECT ON MY SONGWRITING THAT THEY DID."

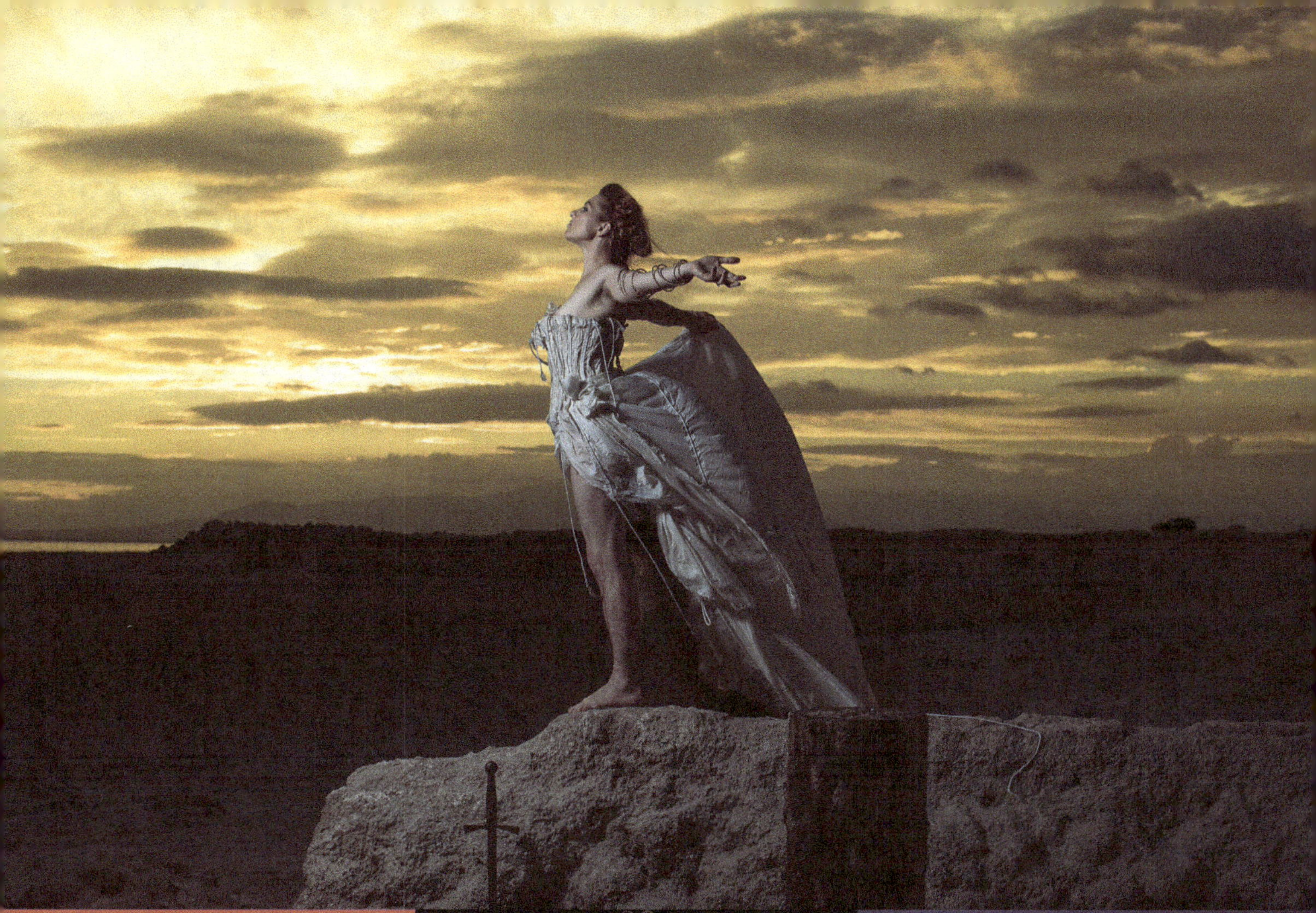

Amanda Loves Magick Magazine

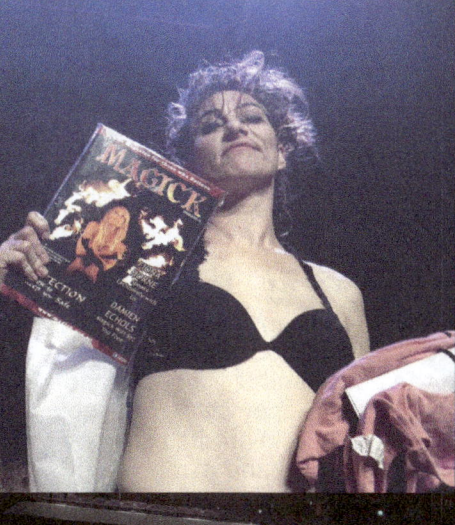

Can you spot your favourite editor in this group chilling with Amanda after her Brisbane Powerhouse gig?

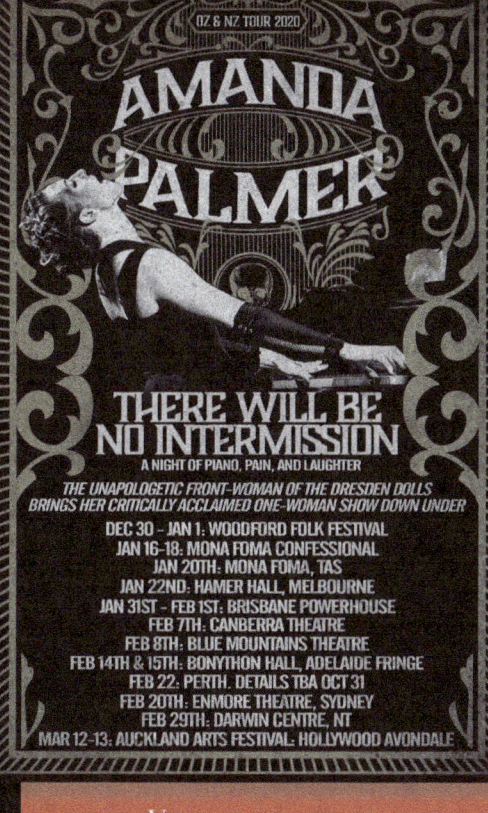

OZ & NZ TOUR 2020
AMANDA PALMER
THERE WILL BE NO INTERMISSION
A NIGHT OF PIANO, PAIN, AND LAUGHTER
THE UNAPOLOGETIC FRONT-WOMAN OF THE DRESDEN DOLLS BRINGS HER CRITICALLY ACCLAIMED ONE-WOMAN SHOW DOWN UNDER
DEC 30 - JAN 1: WOODFORD FOLK FESTIVAL
JAN 16-18: MONA FOMA CONFESSIONAL
JAN 20TH: MONA FOMA, TAS
JAN 22ND: HAMER HALL, MELBOURNE
JAN 31ST - FEB 1ST: BRISBANE POWERHOUSE
FEB 7TH: CANBERRA THEATRE
FEB 8TH: BLUE MOUNTAINS THEATRE
FEB 14TH & 15TH: BONYTHON HALL, ADELAIDE FRINGE
FEB 22: PERTH. DETAILS TBA OCT 31
FEB 20TH: ENMORE THEATRE, SYDNEY
FEB 29TH: DARWIN CENTRE, NT
MAR 12-13: AUCKLAND ARTS FESTIVAL: HOLLYWOOD AVONDALE

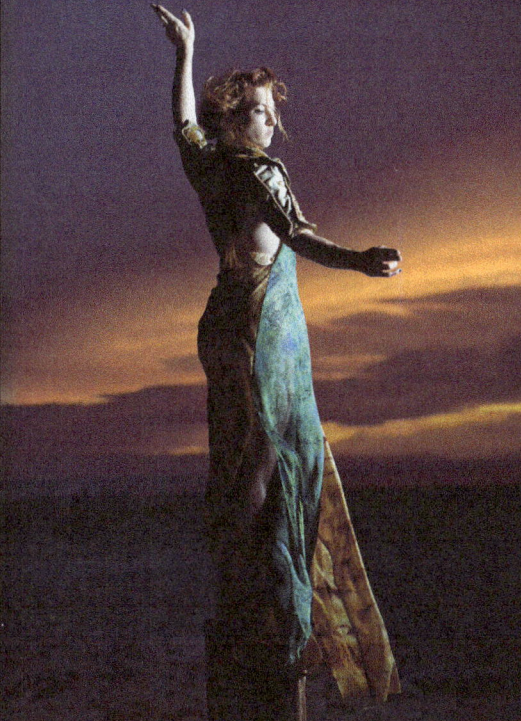

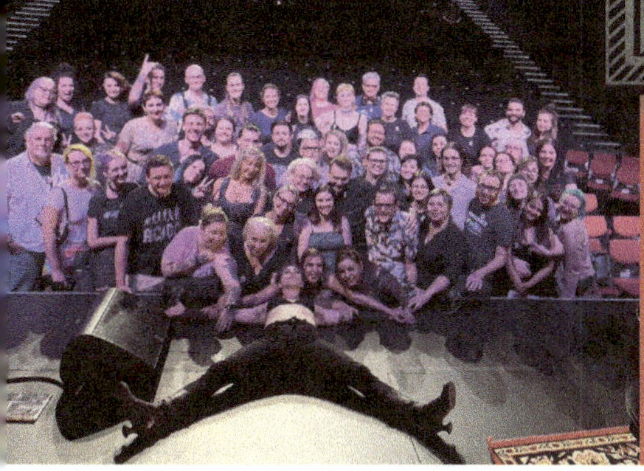

Visit her website and blog at AmandaPalmer.net.
You can listen to Amanda Palmer's book "The Art of Asking." on Audible .com.au
'Drowning In The Sound' film clip:
https://youtu.be/70ApTTyKpdc

AMANDA PALMER
THE ART OF ASKING

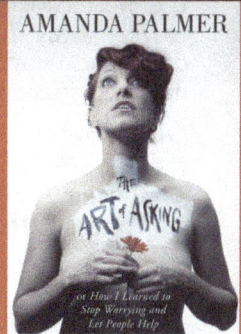

West Country Spells

The south-west of England especially Devon and Cornwall is the birth place of traditional and modern witchcraft practises. Potent examples of the folk-ceremonial magical practices and witchcraft are still apart f daily life. Within the West Country, the popular belief in witchcraft and its attendant charms, magical practices and traditions continued to be observed and survived long after such ways had faded in most other parts of the British Isles.

West Country's cunning folk and witch ways have survived and evolved. Modern day witchcraft practitioners of the old persuasion still practise the ways of the Old Craft and Cunning Arte with include a belief in and working relationship with the spirit forces of the land, the Faerie, animal and plant lore, as well as the magical use of Psalms to cure or curse, the invocation of Christ and the power of the Holy Trinity.

For all those who are interested in learning about the Old Path, as it is taught and practiced today by West Country witches, a visit to The Witchcraft Museum in Boscastle, North Cornwall is enlightening.

The Museum of Witchcraft & Magic (MWM) explores British magical practice, making comparisons with other systems of belief, from ancient times to the present day. We aim to represent the diversity and vigour of magical practice respectfully, accurately and impartially through unique, entertaining and educational exhibitions, drawing upon cutting-edge scholarship along with the insights of magical practitioners. The Museum of Witchcraft & Magic is located by The Harbour in Boscastle, Cornwall. Boscastle is on the North Coast of Cornwall between Tintagel and Bude.

The Museum of Witchcraft & Magic
The Harbour Boscastle Cornwall PL35 0HD
https://museumofwitchcraftandmagic.co.uk

Wortcunning

The Definition of "wortcunning" is: *"The knowledge and use of the secret healing and magickal properties of herbs; a word used by folk healers The West Country of England."*

So any herbal cure is a "Wort." Though they do have a lot of charms for healing worts too.

To Cure a Wort:

Rub the skin of a live toad on the wort then set the toad free, where it will thrive, telling the toad that the wort is a gift you freely give to it. As the toad travels away from the patient over the next few days, the wort will disappear as the toad takes its new "possession" with it.

Steal a potato and cut it in half, rub each half on to the wort. Plant one half and burn the other to ash. As the new potato plant grows from the surviving half portion, the wort will disappear.

Toad Magick

Toad magick is synonymous with West Country magick. Toads, who dwell under and on the earth, who leap high in to the sky as well as diving deep into water; straddled the four realms. They magically metamorph from egg to tadpole to newt and then frog. They can hibernate and live trapped underground for hundreds of years. There are many tales of miners cracking open excavated rocks to release living toads, trapped within for an unimaginable amount of time. They were seen as a Wet Country witch's familiar and friend.

A Toad House Blessing:

At house warming a taod is sent an invitation. One is found and carried to the front door and released. It is let jump through the house and it is hoped that it will find its way through the open back door to the back garden where it will be invited to stay as an honoured guest and be well fed and cared for all of its long life.

If the toad died it was not seen as a bad omen, simply an offering of itself to help with other things. Toads were often mummified and conseald in the structure of the house to bring good luck or parts used in other magick operations. For instance a toad's skull tied with red wool, and kept in the breast pocket, was used as a cure for chest complaints.

Here's a wonderful old reference work that is royalty free and downloadable from the internet:
LEECHDOM & WORTCUNNING -EARLY ENGLAND. - A COLLECTION OF DOCUMENTS, FOR THE MOST PART NEVER BEFORE PRINTED, THE HISTORY OF SCIENCE IN THIS COUNTRY BEFORE THE NORMAN CONQUEST. COLLECTED AND EDITED by REV. OSWALD COCKAYNE, M.A. CANTAB. 1865

JOHN SAFRAN vs THE OCCULT

We asked John Safran why he would dive into investigation of the occult again, after his participation in a Voodou ceremony, that led to his being hypnotised in a mock exorcism by a telly evangelist?

"I've always been intrigued by black magic, which is why I've spent months travelling the globe gathering seemingly impossible stories for my new Audible Original Podcast. They are all modern stories, involving violence and even murder. After I returned home I was surprised to learn how many Australians believe, and dabble, in the occult - although fortunately not the high-end murdery type."

In the podcast, Safran has the courage to investigate a Satanic gang in LA that is condemned by Trump, gets caught up in the politics of sorcery and mob mentality in Vanuatu, and meets a woman in Melbourne who receives an Islamic exorcism to rid herself of a Jinn spirit.

He Exposes Vanuatu's Present-Day Witch Trials & Executions.

"Vanuatu is where small island courts were sentencing people on charges of witchcraft. There were a couple of examples in the last 10 years where these island courts have been used to put people on trial for practising witchcraft, and for the people to be found guilty, and for the people to be sentenced to death and amazing as it sounds, to be put to death."

This offering is not sensationalism and the unthinking dogmatic judgments of other investigative documentaries of "The Craft of the Wise" that we have seen before. John actually tackles issues of magick with humour, yet sensitivity and with rationality, in a way that most practitioners of The Craft would approve. We all know that magick gets used for dark purposes. John examines the ontology, culture and the repercussions of this misuse. A breath of honest fresh air.

I say: "Well done Mr Safran!!" © Shé D'Montford 2020

AYAHUASCA MEDICINE

Ayahuasca Artwork used with permission of Juan Carlos Taminchi https://www.taminchivisions.com

Meeting The Mother On The Mountain: A Day of Unique Happenings

While rumours of this ancient, sacred, and psychoactive brew continue to proliferate within the western narrative, misunderstandings abound even among those who have experienced its profound magic. Expressing this power with speech or text is problematic for two reasons. First of all, the farther one explores reality beyond the five senses, the more difficult it becomes to describe the landscape of the Great Beyond" to others with the instrument of language. Language is composed of a vocabulary that is, by and large, limited to the narrow confines of describing the physical realm. It is therefore nearly impossible to engage in a discourse on the subject of the Great Beyond without immediately becoming saturated in clichés such as, "Whereas once I was blind, now I can see," and so forth, however true they may be. No matter how accurate of a map I am able to draw, it can never accurately portray the subtleties of the immense journey itself.

The other problem associated with writing about Ayahuasca experiences has to do with their sacred nature. Many mystics believe that the spirits of the plants can communicate lessons effectively based on how one learns by virtue of what one knows. Knowledge and wisdom are communicated with intimidating accuracy and lucidity.

The two plants that compose the Ayahuasca brew are *Psychotria viridis* (or *charuna*: the leaf of light) and *Banisteriopsis caapi* (the vine of strength). Together, they create an intelligence whose depth immensely transcends what our human minds can rationalise. Their wisdom is revered with such solemn reverence that it is considered disrespectful to verbally curse or even hold negative intentions near the brew.

Ayahuasca that I have brewed myself the past I often refer to as "white-boy brew." For someone not of the native lineage, even if I follow the method precisely and keep my intentions genuinely pure, it will never be as potent as a brew charged with the skilful intentions of a seasoned medicine-man. Just as one must incorporate love into food while cooking it, there is so much more at work here than merely the chemistry of the physical ingredients.

By no means a recreational experience, Amazonian medicine-men refer to the brew as the "Little Death". Through the experience, one faces their own mortality, temporarily crossing over to the other side while still inhabiting a human body. One grows to know their fears on a surprising level, and is given the opportunity to face and overcome them like a charging locomotive bearing down upon the mind. This is one of the most important experiences an individual can have in their lifetime, so it is therefore important to get every single detail exactly correct, in the same way that one only takes flight in an airplane that has been properly maintained, checked, and serviced.

I liken the experience to cleaning one's house. Our focus in the west is so external that we seldom pay much attention to our own temples. We are fundamentally fearful of holding the mirror up to ourselves because we're intuitively aware of the messes within, and it is easier to look away from them than to deal with them. Bad habits, energetic imbalances, resentment, jealousy, vanity, guilt, and other impurities are the clutters that pile up regularly within everyone, but if left unchecked will eventually begin to compromise the integrity of the temple itself. Many people understand that physical diseases are manifestations of psychological, emotional, and spiritual schisms. The incentive to do that hard work seems rather intuitive, but the perception of it as "work" lends itself quite naturally to procrastination. But cleaning one's temple isn't just hard work; it is an inherently playful act because a clean house is pleasing both to oneself and one's guests. The work may seem difficult in the short term, but in the end you're always glad you did it because everything is lighter, friendlier, and better organised. In the same way that cleaning the house requires effort and a willingness to embrace the filth, true healing requires an expansive undertaking of one's own inner darkness. Still, this is easier said than done. We are all more afraid than we may like to admit, and many of us choose to put off the ultimate question until the eleventh hour. I've heard it said that those who wait until the eleventh hour to contemplate the deep questions actually shine out at 10:30. In this way, drinking Ayahuasca is like having your mother come to your house and lovingly criticise every stain, spill, and mess while helping you make sense of it all as you frantically try to keep up.

It is accurate to assert that many different methods are capable of yielding experiences of cosmic consciousness, and they're by no means limited to encounters with entheogenic compounds. Yogic breathing exercises and meditative absorptions are also capable of yielding states of consciousness similar to that of Ayahuasca. Mystics seek these states for their revelatory potentials; they are capable of apportioning wisdom, healing, prophecy, and manifestation to the careful practitioner. But while alternate methods are capable of yielding very similar states of consciousness, only the Ayahuasca brew is capable of delivering one into communion with Mother Ayahuasca herself.

After meticulous preparation and an extensive journey into the Rocky Mountain wilderness, I was ready to face the Ineffable within a sacred mountain paradise. There was just one problem. After 18 months of good health I fell deeply ill just days ago, and haven't had the energy to do much of anything. With one day remaining on this magical group retreat, I'm deeply troubled by this downturn of heath, fearing that it may prevent the full potential of the visionary experience. But this morning it suddenly occurred to me that if Ayahuasca is a medicine powerful enough to overcome cancerous tumours, it could probably help with whatever virus I've picked up. Though I must say, addressing the flu with Ayahuasca is tantamount to killing a mosquito with a cannonball. Given the seriousness of the undertaking, I've stalled drinking so that I might be as strong as possible because, counter to the methodology of western medicine, you certainly don't need to be sick to imbibe medicine. True medicine heals multiple facets of one's being, and this particular experience is absolutely exhausting. So I made up my mind to seize the day's potential, and instead of eating breakfast I measured ten ounces of brew and poured it into Electra's kettle to warm in our fire pit. Once it started to steam, I poured it into a cup and walked to the lake's shore beneath a mighty spruce tree. Here, I took the ancient medicine sip by sip as the rippling waves danced toward me.

As a disclaimer I must tell you that a solitary experience with Ayahuasca is not necessarily recommended. These journeys are typically undertaken in groups with the aid of a very experienced guide (which I myself have undergone many times previously). For one thing, it is emotionally reassuring to have others around you in case you encounter something you don't know how to deal with. This particular experience was guided by an intention to bring the healing spirit of Mother Ayahuasca into familiar mountains close to my own relations, and I feel that I was given a specific permission to take the risk of a solitary journey, as it was accompanied with a moral contract that I would bear the responsibility of conveying the knowledge that was gained. I felt a certain permission, and even duty, to communicate the experience I'm about to express. I am certain that something conveyed herein is capable of helping heal the world, and never has there been a more precarious or desperate time in our history for such knowledge.

I finished my serving and laid down on the rocks. Waves of energy welled up, beginning first at my feet. A familiar desperation climbed into my stomach, much like the slow ascent of a rollercoaster clicking up the main rise. My upper body was in the sunshine, though my clothes prevented my skin from absorbing the rays. The thought occurred to me that I might be able to more fully appreciate today's lesson if I embraced nature as though I were a part of her instead of trying to shield myself from her, embracing unity rather than duality. So, I unbuttoned the top buttons of my white dress shirt, soon finding the task intellectually challenging while my consciousness began to flutter beyond the five senses. When my shirt was finally unbuttoned, I found the sun searing on my chest but was too overwhelmed to fiddle with my clothes any longer. It was time to focus, relax, and surrender. I decided that I would learn to accept the sun's hotness and interpret the burning sensation as the absorption of light.

Then came the flies. Swarms of carnivorous flies appeared all around. Biting my flesh they buzzed about, swarming around my spinning head. While the horseflies themselves were indeed physical creatures, my mind was starting to enter visionary territory beyond the physical plane. Kaleidoscopic fractals swirled in brilliant colours while the flies picked at my chest. I tried to wave them off but found myself immediately apologetic to the creatures; the thought of killing them made me sick. My first thought was that this must be how it felt for those who have died in the wilderness, full of desperate anxiety, hot and uncomfortable, about to make the ultimate transition while still aware of a rotting body of flesh no longer suitable for anything but feeding hungry flies... and eventually vultures and coyotes.

A gentle breeze quickly transformed into a persistent wind. As my mind thrashed for clarity, the increasing winds seemed to reflect my inner distress. It blew harder and harder until the fir trees were howling, their branches whipping to and fro in the torrent. The whole forest began to shriek. The calm ripples on the water reversed direction and the lake seemed to boil. Pebbles were lifted from the beach and tossed about. My internal fears seemed fiercely projected into the external world. What began to look like a storm made me reach into my lungs for a scream. I gasped panicked breaths. When the winds reached fever-pitch I noticed that the hurricane of activity had drawn away all of the tormenting flies. Immediately upon realising this, the air began to synchronistically calm and within moments the forest was once again peaceful.

Electra's familiar voice emerged from the trees. She knelt down beside me and asked how I was doing. I searched for words, but operating my left-brain was out of the question. As I tried, colour and depth began to fade while my guts turned. I opened my mouth to respond but words didn't come out. Instead I keeled over and vomited onto the mossy beach into an earthen divot. Electra put a hand on my slumped shoulder and uttered an exclamation under her breath. Her growing concern for me was creating a vibrational dissonance that was perceivably uncomfortable because I could feel what she was feeling on a very deep level. In an attempt to reassure her, I conjured the only words I could, "No... It's beautiful."

The Two Plants That Compose the Ayahuasca Brew

Psychotria viridis or *charuna*: The Leaf of Light

Banisteriopsis caapi: The Vine of Strength

It *was* astonishingly beautiful. The purge had liberated inner darkness, expelled the sickness, and removed negativity from every fibre of my being. Every cell of the world was dancing in celebration. Everything was right on schedule. A physical purging usually accompanies the imbibition of Ayahuasca and is actually desirable. In fact it is very unusual not to purge.

The grasses were waving back and forth, and I could clearly see a unifying life-force shimmering within everything that was alive. Every blade of grass and every pine needle glowed with a singular pulse like individual cells composing something larger than the sum of their parts. It was the essence of life that flows through the entirety of the universe. All that is alive resonates with this force, for the universe is one massive organism. All living organisms vibrated, shimmered and sang together in brilliant choreography.

Electra said she was going to search for the knife she'd lost yesterday on the other side of the lake near the falls. The word "knife" opened doors I didn't want to explore, so I just nodded and laid my head down on the beach with a groan. Peering directly upward through the foliage of a magnificent spruce, the branches began throbbing with pulsating beams of life and singing divine songs.

Then something completely alien overwhelmed my senses. In lonely desperation I called out, "Electra?" It was the whimper of an infant, insecure and fearful, but nobody could hear it. The surrounding cliffs melted like living oil paintings as my physical presence rapidly evaporated. As the "I" of ego ceased to be, whatever remained of "me" surrounded my body, no longer confined to the sensory limits of the nervous system. As sensations diffused, so too did all the abstract notions of ego: defilements of guilt, anger, delusion, jealousy, and vanity all dissolved in the rising etheric mist.

Feeling much lighter, I arose to a cross-legged position and began to hum a low tone across the dancing waters. I could clearly perceive the greater organism of which we are all a part. I could no longer interpret individual plants as separate from each other, nor perceive the lake's waves as distinct from the grasses on the shore, nor pebbles from roots. One major pulse steadily pumped life through All That Is. Everything from the stones to the clouds was alive with this energy.

Near the waterfall across the lake, Electra climbed down to the far shore. Her movements became part of this harmonised spiritual process. She was not climbing down a steep embankment; she was as much a part of that embankment as she was the grasses and trees upon it, all of which swayed together with choreographed accuracy.

As my constitution grew stronger, my humming grew louder. I began to hum with an open mouth, and then began throat-singing. The vibrations aligned every cell in my body, and Mother Ayahuasca began to speak. *You cannot attain it*, she communicated, but the geometry of this message was more complex than just that. The various nuances of her lesson were telepathically downloaded. *Since we are all greedy for experience, the drive to attain is strong within us,* I was told. In a multitude of ways, she continued to reiterate that there is nothing in life that can truly be attained.

Everything in existence is unattainable. Neither the water in your bottle nor that in your veins is really yours. Every drop must eventually be returned. Even your body. You cannot attain it because there is no you. There is only this beautiful process, or there is the lack of it. You are made of water and are thus part of the process unless you choose not to be. Such a choice leads to disease.

These messages caused me to reflect on the archetype of the wounded healer, who learns how to heal others by himself experiencing the very diseases that must be combated. He must learn how to heal himself before being of any use to others in a healing capacity. Throughout the process of my singing, my sinuses leaked mucous profusely. The louder and longer I sang, the more easily the air flowed through my passages. Mother Ayahuasca explained to me that while she was herself a healer, all she could really do was empower me with the ability to understand how to harness my own immune system. After all, nobody knows it better or uses it more frequently than I. In exactly the same way, nobody can breathe or beat my heart for me. Every perceivable function of the human body is inescapably personal even if one falsely believes it to be "automatic."

According to this visionary communication, the misbelief that we lack control over our own bodies allows sicknesses to overtake us. No medication or healer can take control of one's own immune system. Nothing will ever do it *for* us, though we constantly push this responsibility on drugs and doctors. Such a choice can lead to perverted healing and eventually more mysterious sicknesses. We must do it ourselves if it is to be proper. And in this way I can see how even the strongest diseases are a product of mental susceptibility. But if they are a product of the mind, so is the cure.

The world is sick. The present corporate hegemony demands obedience and passivity. This mentality distorts the human organism into a vessel that is susceptible to diseases and maladies of all kinds. As above, so below. Our state of mind instructs our cells. If we cultivate courage, so will the cells of our bodies. If we strive each day to achieve the impossible, our cells will follow suit. If we are determined to give up, our cells will feel this disharmony and give up themselves, opening the door to a variety of disease to which we would otherwise be immune. Dauntless spirits grow indomitable immune systems, while a composure of victimisation leads to weakened health. This deep magic is a part of how the human vessel operates within our experience of reality.

My Ayahuasca visions were beginning to recede. The journey came full-circle upon a fascinating observation. I perceived those carnivorous flies for their true role in the dance of life: these seemingly vicious little creatures are in fact directly harmonised with the frequency of nature; her humming immune cells constantly cleansing the excrement of the forest.

Author: Gabrielle Lafayette

is a native Montanan on a lifelong quest to heal this planet and inspire others to do the same. To achieve these ends, he produces broadcast journalism, professional ink Mandalas, full-length concept albums, as well as philosophical reflections as apportioned from guiding individuals and groups through psychedelic experiences and meditative absorptions

---

Artist: Juan Carlos Taminchi

is a young Peruvian artist who has inherited from the Andean and Amazonian cultures. At 8 years old, the surrounding nature drew his attention and stimulated his drawing abilities, and thus opened the possibilities to artistic dreaming. In college, he attended a drawing class that inspired him to study art at the Pucallpa School of Arts, where he then became an Art Professor. From the age of 17, searching for his artistic style, he discovered the spirit world and sacred plants, which enabled him to deepen his approach to Visionary Art – a sacred and spiritual gift given by Mother Earth. He took part in several exhibits and attended several workshops with other visionary artists from his area. In October 2009, he made his first individual art exhibit that was named "Amazonia" in Paris France. Later, he acted on behalf of an association of Amazonian painters and sculptors called ONANYATI, which means "Wisdom from Ancestors" in the Shipibo language in the collective exhibit "Jamais trop d'art" in Tournai, Belgium. He also took part in various exhibitions such as "Third Eye Gallery"-Boom Festival 2012 in Portugal, "Burning Man 2012," "Matices de las Americas", "Moksha Fair Art-2012"- Miami U.S, "Chimera 2014"- Sedan- France, Symbiosis Festival 2015, California- U.S and many other exhibitions in Europe and the Americas. Since 2012, he has dedicated his life to serving and sharing the sacred medicine of Amazon, and also leading shamanic art- therapy workshops in various spiritual events. He is often invited to do live painting in events and concerts all around the globe. https://www.taminchivisions.com

Fellow Travellers for the Goddess

Many people believe that walking the Camino de Compostela opens them to life-changing personal and spiritual experiences powered by the energy from the Milky Way above and the millions who have trodden the earthly path below. There are many people whose lives have been completely transformed by this journey across Spain. Open-hearted love, overcome by tears of joy, wonder or gratitude are the soul's natural response to the incredible natural, architectural beauty and energy of the Ancient Celtic sites in the north of Spain on this track. It is a recognised Catholic pilgrimage and there are facilities set up to help pilgrims all along this track. Though it is currently claimed as a Catholic pilgrimage, we know that pilgrims have been walking this track, longer than the Catholic Church has been in existence. Regardless of religion, on this sacred pilgrimage, walkers experience goodwill, kindness, openness and warmth within the group of fellow travellers and from the communities transversed on this journey. It really is a magickal journey, a courageous mortal who is returning to the source, whilst watching the stars of the Milky Way twinkling overhead every night.

Get In Touch With The Oldest Celtic Roots. There was a huge Celtic migration from this Iberian Peninsula to Ireland & Scotland in pre-christian times. They took with them an Egyptian princess/priestess called Scota, after whom Scotland was named. In fact, the Gaelic language/culture is named after Gaelitia, the the largest area with the most pagan artefacts on the walk. The pilgrimage retraces the path of that Celtic migration (of the Milesians & Gaels) under the path of the Milkey Way to meet the goddess Nimah who will take you to the fairy realm. The Camino is ancient and sacred. It is full of power. Walking the path is transformative. It changes you.

If you walk this crocked and winding path Magick will happen!

- Buen Camino

YOUR PERSONAL INVITATION

Corvid19 restrictions permitting - Come **JOIN US** on a trip to The Camino on Sept 1 2021 which we will be organising for some of our readers. Find the origins of all Celtic culture as we journey on a 780 km walk starting from St Jean Pied de Port, on the 1st of September. Because there is filming, we will take 35 days to walk the trail which is only 22^{km} per day. Older participants are advised to do some walking and take cabs between towns. If you can afford to take a month for yourself, **It will be a transformative once in a lifetime experience.** The Camino is free to walk but you will still have to pay your own airfares, accommodation and food - which is very reasonably priced.

PLAN & PREPARE - If you would like to accompany us please do some more research. People who have done The Camino are happy to blog about it online and there is a lot of advise & lots of guide books.

Magick Magazine is making a documentary about The Camino and you can be part of this too!
We are fundraising for this project. So if you would like to come with us please make a donation and we will help you organise this trip. Even if you can't come with us it would be great if you could be part of making such a worthy goddess filled documentary. Because Magick Magazine is part of a Pagan charitable organisation, any donation is tax deductible. If you would like to register to walk with us may you find it in your heart to donate via the:

Fellow Travellers for The Goddess eventbrite link here https://fellowtravelersforthegoddess.eventbrite.com.au
or Donate directly via Paypal https://shambhallah.wordpress.com/donate

Council Sponsors Fairytales & Folklore

The peoples choice winner
Kristie Faulkner
The Light Princess
Photography on fine art paper

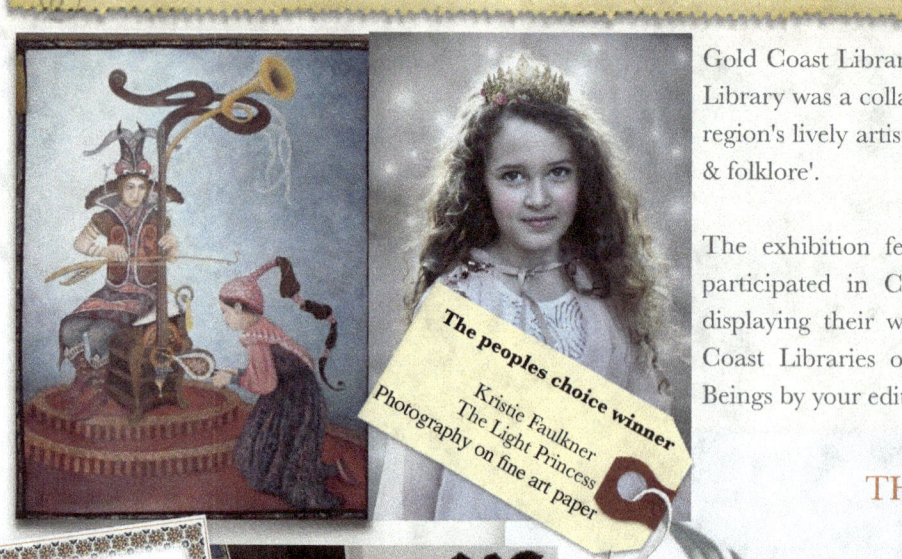

Gold Coast Libraries' annual artist exhibition August 2019, Robina Library was a collaborative exhibition showcasing artworks from the region's lively artistic community, under this year's theme 'Fairy tales & folklore'.

The exhibition features Gold Coast artists who have previously participated in City Libraries' Artist Showcase' program, either displaying their work and/or as an 'Artist in Residence' at Gold Coast Libraries over the past few years.This included 2 Goetic Beings by your editor, Shé D'Montford

THE DEER HUNTER

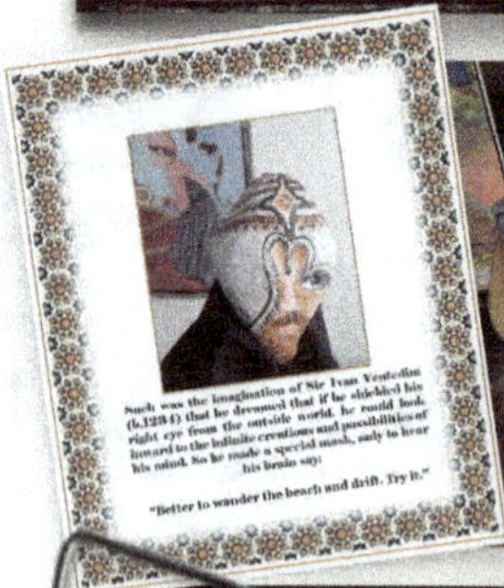

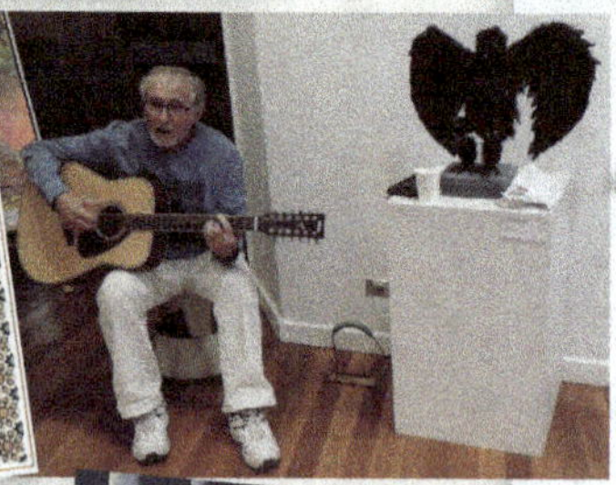

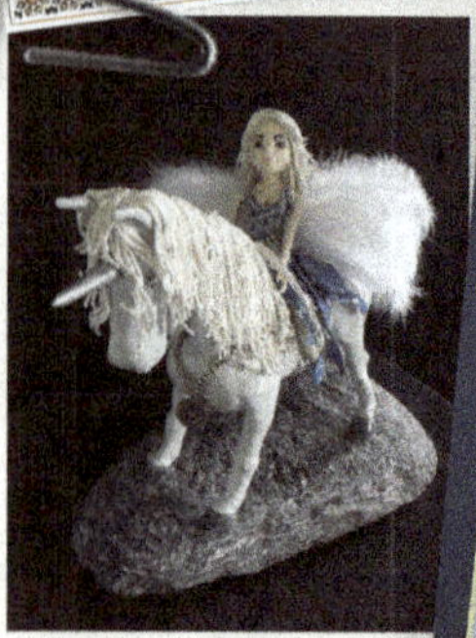

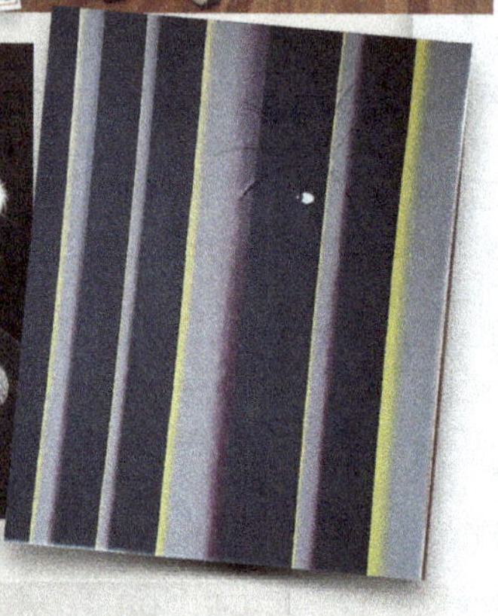

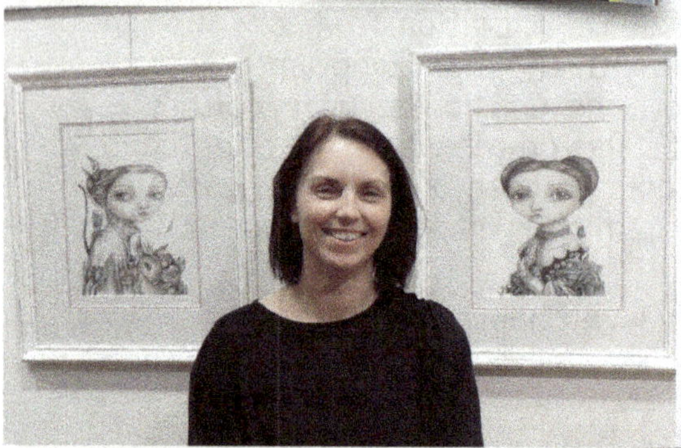

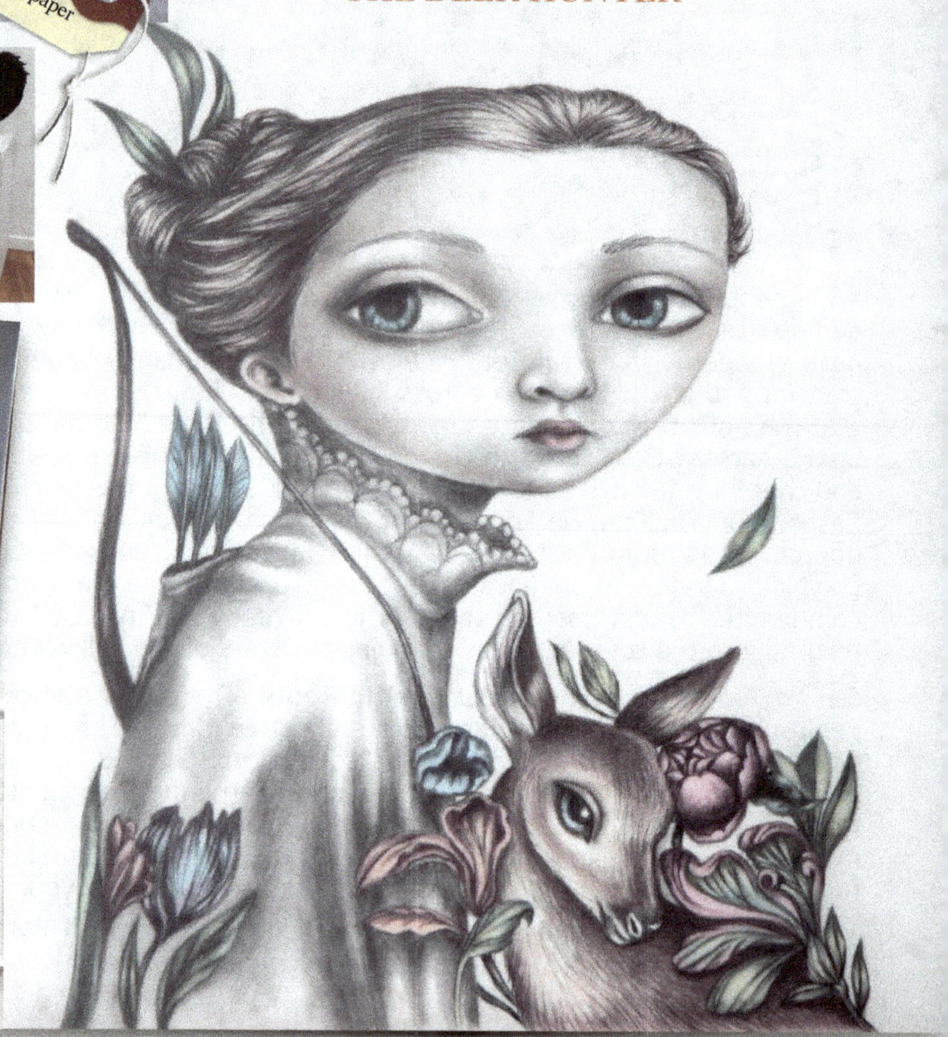

MAGICK MAGAZINE

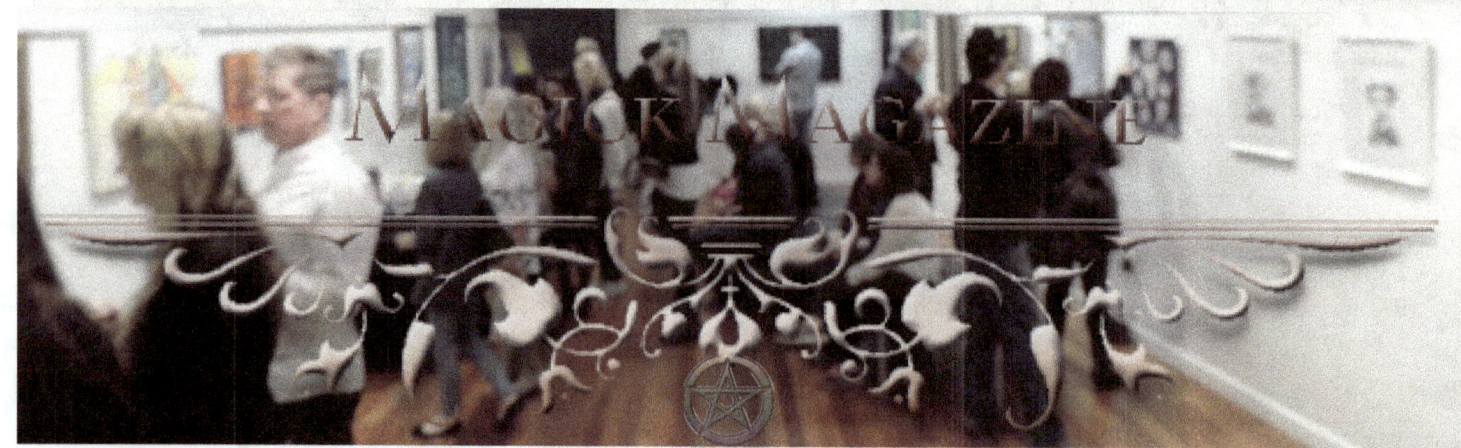

The Islamic Greenman

The Magickal Mystic

Al-Khiḍr, is the legendary immortal prophet, mystic, trickster and sea spirit. Khiḍr literally means 'The Green One,' he is always depicted as wearing green and sometimes with green skin. Though he appears in both the Hindu and Islamic traditions, al-Khiḍr is widely known as the spiritual guide of Moses and Alexander the Great, a wali (saint), a prophet, and one of four immortals along with Enoch (Idris), Jesus, and Elijah. He was magickal and performed many miracles. He is popular amongst Sufis in Turkey and Sri Lanka and has become the Patron Saint of Cannabis.

In Muslim tradition, Green represents fertility, femininity and new life. It is the sacred colour of that belief system. It is easy to see how sacred green could be to a faith that has its origins in the deep desert. For this tradition green represents freshness of spirit and eternal liveliness, the freshness of knowledge *"drawn out of the living sources of life."* Whatever the source for this green may be, it has come to symbolise the benign presence of wisdom as imparted by the Divine Himself to Khiḍr and to Prophet Muhammad.

Qur'ān commentators say that al-Khiḍr is one of the prophets; others refer to him simply as an angel who functions as a guide to those who seek God. Others argue for his being a perfect wali, meaning the one whom God has taken as a friend.

Khiḍr is associated with the Water of Life. Since he drank the water of immortality he is described as the one who has found the source of life, 'The Eternal Youth.' He is the mysterious guide and immortal saint in popular Islamic lore and the hidden initiator of those who walk the mystical path.

In the Islamic tradition Khiḍr is a living being. He's alive and well and continues to guide the perplexed and those who invoke his name.

In Western Asia, Moslem & Hindu symbolic art shows the Saint, Al Khizr, dressed in a green coat being carried on top of the water by a fish which conveys him over the river of life.

Khiḍr - "The Verdant One"
Plays a pivotal role in Islamic mysticism.
As stated in Sura 18 (*al-Kahf*) of the Holy Qur'ān.

Spell To Meet The Greenman

This prayer is recited in order to meet Hadrat Khiḍr (Alahi Salām) who appears in a dream and advises the supplicator.
* Say this prayer last thing before going to bed.
* Go to bed without conversing with anyone after reciting this prayer.
* First read any darood (prayers of praise) 11 times.
* Then read the following prayer 15 times.
* Then end with recitation of the darood 11 times.
* Then ask Allah arrange the meeting.
* Lie down and fall asleep on the right side of the body.

Bismillah hir Rahman nir Raheem
Bismillah hir Rahman nir Raheem
Bismillahi al Amān al Amān
Ya Hanān al Amān al Amān
Ya Manān al Amān al Amān
Ya da Yān al Amān al Amān
Ya subhan al Amān al Amān
Ya burhān al Amān al Amān
Min fitna tiz zAmāni wa jafā
Il ikhwani wa shar rish shaitan
Wa zulmis sultan be fadhlika
Ya Raheem Ya Rahman
Ya zul Jalāli wal ikrām
Wa sall Allahu ala khairi khaliqi
hi Muhammadin wa alihi wa as hābi hi ajmaeen bi Rahmatika
Ya Arham ar Rahimeen
Wa sall Allahu ala Khairi
Khaliqi Hi Muhammadin
wa alihi wa as Hābi
hi Ajmaeen bi Rahmatika
Ya Arham Ar Rahimeen

JOEY POTTER

PAGAN 3D ARTIST

Joey Potter has shared with us her Goblin punk mask, journal spreads and monster mural.

Artist bio:
Joey Potter, post apocalyptic mischief maker, collector of bells, bones and old medicine, tooth puller, tinkerer, pedlar of monsters, machines and other whirligigs n whatnots, a strange, scribbled in bit of monster marginalia in a medieval bestiary posing as human, protector of those who narrowly escape disaster, local menace.

See more of Joey Potter's work on her Instagram

She is available for commissions by contacting her on her email **joey.s.potter98@gmail.com**

HERMETIC INVOCATION TO APHRODITE GODDESS OF LOVE

VENUS

22	47	16	41	10	35	4
5	23	48	17	42	11	29
30	6	24	49	18	36	12
13	31	7	25	43	19	37
38	14	32	1	26	44	20
21	39	8	33	2	27	45
46	15	40	9	34	3	28

Hermetic Magick is an accurate recreation of the ancient magickal rituals practised in Egypt and Greece in the 3rd and 4th centuries just before it was finally outlawed by the power of the new Church of Rome. Performing this kind of Magick puts us directly in contact with powerful archetypal egregores. These invocations are taken from the Greek Magickal Papyrus, and presented here exactly as it would have been performed in 3rd and 4th century Alexandria. To perform a Hermetic ritual:-

1. Pick a celestially auspicious time that is in harmony with the desired changes that you seek to produce. Referring to the Almanac may help you determine when is the best time to perform these rites for your specific needs.
2. Perform the 'Ancient Hermetic Opening Rite'
3. Perform the 'Deity Invocation' using the corresponding magick square, deity image, colours, hymns, incense and oil.
4. Once the energy comes in, you can simply commune with it, make a request or perform a spell.
5. Perform the 'Ancient Hermetic Closing Rite'

Know The God You Are Invoking

There are a number of myths concerning the origins of Aphrodite. Due to space constrains we shall only consider Hesiod's writings, where Aphrodite is transformed from the patroness of an Anatolian city in the Alti-Caucasus called Aphrodisias, that was still a prosperous city during the Roman Empire. There she was more than a mere fertility Goddess, she was also aspected to all things beautiful, including art, science and philosophy. She has always been associated with the creative and destructive aspects of love.

In Hesiod's "Theogony," the world emerges from chaos, followed by the birth of the 12 Titans, whose parents were Ouranos, the sky, and Gaia, the earth. Unprepared for the responsibilities of fatherhood, Ouranos hides his offspring inside Gaia's body. In pain, Gaia cries out for help, whereupon Kronos, the youngest, responds by castrating Ouranos and tossing his genitals into the Mediterranean Sea. The genitals are enveloped in a mist of white foam from which a beautiful maiden appears. She was transported on a scallop shell to the Greek island, Kythera where she was called Kytherea. She then travels to Cyprus, where she was first worshipped, and is named Aphrodite, which means "she who comes from foam." When she first walks on Cypriot soil, grass springs up under her feet and she is affirmed as a fertility goddess who revitalises the earth.

Aphrodite's temple at Corinth was renowned for its priestesses who performed initiation rites and provided sexual services to incoming sailors. As time went on, Aphrodite's role of a Goddess of love overshadowed her role as a fertility deity. In Hesiod's "Works and Days", Zeus assigns the roles of the Olympic deities. Aphrodite's role is that of goddess of love and beauty, while her former role as a goddess of agriculture is given to Demeter.

It is interesting to note that Venus rules both Libra and Taurus. Aphrodite's role as a goddess of love and beauty arising from balance is certainly compatible with her rulership of Libra. However, her rulership over Taurus suggests that we should be mindful also of her original role as an unstoppable force, impulsive, passionate, destructive and a potently fertile Goddess.

Aphrodite is commonly called up for workings involving love, graciousness, beauty, success in romance, the arts that are associated with the physical as well as science, mathematics and philosophy, which associates her with the beautiful mind. The goal of this working is to experience the real goddess energy behind the myths of Aphrodite. If you have any concerns with love (or agriculture for that matter!) this working will be a good opportunity to have those concerns addressed.

Colour: Green

Metal: Copper

Sent: Spike Nard, Indian Nard, Rose

Numbers: 7 49, 175 and 1225:
- Each row & column of her magic square contains 7 numbers.
- The square contains 49 numbers total, 1-49
- Each row, column and diagonal adds up to 175.
- All of the numbers in the square add up to 1225.

The Opening Ritual   From the PGM XXXVI. 312 - 20

"Open up for me, open up for me, door; be opened, be opened, door,
Because I am Horus the Great,
ARCHEPHRENEPSOU PHIYRIGX,
Child of Osiris and Isis.
Immediately, immediately; quickly, quickly."   Tr.: R. F. Hock.

The Instruction: From PGM XIII. 7341077
EAST - Stretching out your right hand to the left and your left hand likewise to the left, say "A."
NORTH - Putting forward only your right fist, say "E."
WEST - Extending both hands in front of you, say " Ē."
SOUTH - Holding both on your stomach, say, "I"
EARTH -The point below PAST
Bending over, touching the ends of your toes, say "O."
MID POINT – starting in front of you - the here and now (The Point pf power is in the present moment)
Having your hand on your heart, say "Y."
SKY - The Point Above - FUTURE
Having both hands on your head, say "Ō"

"I call on you, eternal and unbegotten, who are one, who alone hold together the whole creation of all things, whom none understands, whom the gods worship, whose name not even the gods can utter. Inspire from your exhalation ruler of the pole, him who is under you; accomplish for me the what ever I request

I call on you as by the voice of the male gods,
IĒŌ OYE ŌĒI YE AŌ EI ŌY AOĒ OYĒ EŌA YĒI ŌEA OĒŌ IEOU AŌ.

I call on you, as by the voice of the female gods,
IAĒ EŌO IOY EĒI ŌA EĒ IĒ AI YO ĒIAY EŌO OYĒE IAŌ ŌAI EOYĒ YŌĒI IŌA

I call on you, as the winds call you.
I call on you, as the dawn." (Looking toward East say)
"A EE ĒĒĒ IIII OOOOO YYYYY ŌŌŌŌŌŌŌ"

"I call on you as the south." (Looking to the south say)
"I OO YYY ŌŌŌŌ AAAAA EEEEEE ĒĒĒĒĒĒĒ"

"I call on you as the west." (Looking to the west, say)
"Ē II OOO YYY ŌŌŌŌŌ AAAAAA EEEEEEE"

"I call on you as the north." (Looking to the north say)
"Ō AA EEE ĒĒĒĒ IIIII ŌŌŌŌŌŌ YYYYYYY"

"I call on you / as the earth." (Looking to the earth say)
"E ĒĒ III OOO YYYYY ŌŌŌŌŌŌ AAAAAAA"

I call on you as the sky." (Looking into the sky say)
"Y ŌŌ AAA EEEE ĒĒĒĒĒ IIIIII OOOOOOO"

I Call on you as the cosmos,
(Looking straight ahead into the middle distance)
"O YY ŌŌŌ AAAA EEEEE ĒĒĒĒĒĒ IIIIIII"

Accomplish for me whatever I ask quickly.
I call on your name, the greatest among gods.
I call on you, IYEYO ŌAEĒ IAŌ AEĒ AI EĒ AĒ IOYŌ EYĒ IEOU AĒŌ ĒI ŌĒI IAĒ IŌOYĒ AYĒ YĒA 1Ō   IŌAI IŌAI ŌĒ EE OY 1Ō IAŌ, the great name.

Become for me lynx, eagle, snake, phoenix, life power, necessity, images of god,
AIŌ IŌY IAO ĒIŌ AA OYI AAAA E IY IŌ OĒ IAŌ AI AŌIĒ OYEŌ AIEĒ IOYE YEIA EIŌ ĒII YY EE ĒĒ ŌAŌĒ CHECHAMPSIMM CHANGALAS
EEIOY IĒEA OOĒOE seven of the auspicious names
ZŌIŌIĒR ŌMYRYROMROMOS"
"Ē II YY ĒĒ OAOĒ."

HERMETIC APHRODITE INVOCATION

O foam-bone Kythercia, mother of both gods and men, ethereal and chthonic, AR, Mother Nature, goddess unsubdued, who hold together things, who cause the great fire to revolve, who keep the ever-moving BARZA in her unbroken course., and you accomplish everything, from head to toes, and by your will is holy water mixed, when by your hands you'll move RHOUZ amid the stars, the world's midpoint which you control. You move holy desire into the souls of men and move woman to man, and you render woman desirable to man. But, if as goddess you in slowness act, you will not see Adonis rise from Hades, straightway I'll run and bind him with steel chains, as guard, I'll bind on him another wheel of Ixion; No longer will he come to light, and he'll be chastised and subdued... Wherefore, O Lady, act, I beg: at once, quickly.   For I adjure you, Kythere;" NOUMILLON; BIOMBILLON; AKTIOPHI;   ERESCHIGAL; NEBOUTOSOUALETH; PHROU; REXIA; THERMIDOCHE; BAREO-NE."Through all the days to come, our Goddess Queen, come to these chants, Mistress ARRORIPHRASI, GOTHETINI, Cyprus-born, SOUIEE; THNOBOCHOU; THORITHE STHENEPIO, Lady SERTHENEBEEI... but, blessed RHOUZO, grant this to me, (your name) just as into your chorus 'mid the stars. A man unwilling you attracted to your bed for intercourse, and once he was attracted, he at once began to turn, great BARZA, nor did he cease turning, and while moving in his circuits, he's aroused: But goddess Cyprus-born, do you now, to the full, fulfil this chant.

Closing Ritual   From the PGM XXXVI. 312 - 20

"Close up for me, Close up for me, door; be locked, be barred, door, until I open you again.
Because I am Horus the Great,
ARCHEPHRENEPSOU PHIYRIGX,
Child of Osiris and Isis.
Immediately, immediately; quickly, quickly." Tr.: R. F. Hock.
The Instruction: From PGM XIII. 7341077
SKY - The Point Above - FUTURE
Having both hands on your head, say "Ō"
MID POINT – Strand in front of you - the here and now (The Point of power is in the present moment)
Having your hand on your heart, say "Y."
EARTH -The point below PAST
Bending over, touching the ends of your toes, say "O."
SOUTH - Holding both on your stomach, say, "I"
WEST - Extending both hands in front of you, say " Ē."
NORTH - Putting forward only your right fist, say "E."
EAST- Stretching out your right hand to the left and your left hand likewise to the left, say "A."

Upon performing this Hermetic invocation, the Aphrodite energy will come into the ritual immediately, and it has been our experience that the effects of invoking this egregore will continue to manifest in your life for approximately 1 month. Therefore, it is not recommended that you perform any more than one rite per month so that you can observe the changes that being on intimate terms with this new energy will bring into your life. Everywhere it has been performed we have seen that the effects of this ritual is not subjective but can be objectively observed and accurately repeated. This ritual is powerful and will produce the expected results for the solitary practitioner or coven that chooses to perform it. As this God-force energy is connected with the planet Venus, information in the almanac will help you to determine how she is aspected and when is the best time to perform this ritual for your specific needs. "Magic Classes" in this magazine over the ensuing issues will teach you the basic methods involved in performing these ceremonies correctly. Use them wisely and for a high purpose.

© Copyright Rev. Dr. S. D'Montford, Saturday 7th August 1999 Gold Coast. Australia

Rev. Dr. S'D'Montford began performing these hermetic invocations taken directly from the Greek Magical Papyri, 25 years ago, with Barrington Vincent Sherman, half a decade before others began to try to copy her magickal work in this field. For those interested in being initiated into this magickal order, to learn the subtleties needed to meet with & work with these powerful archetypes to transform your life, you can contact us through:

www.magick.org.au

PAMELA COLEMAN-SMITH

The Myth and Mystery of this Amazing Magickal Woman

The Rider-Waite deck, was published in December 1909 and went on to become the most popular tarot deck in the world. Though the beloved images on the cards have become a collective consciousness archetype, the artist behind them has received little recognition. Until recently, her name was left off most editions of the deck. These erasures accompany recurrent questions about Colman-Smith.

Who Was Pamela Coleman-Smith?
Pamela Colman-Smith (16 February 1878 - 18 September 1951 age 73) was a woman ahead of her time. She is popularly remember for being the artist for the Rider-Wait dec. Yes, her tarot was an important part of her career, yet she is also a great figure that championed issues that are percolating to the surface of society now in the early 21th century. Things like: gender equality, race and identity and really thriving in traditionally male held spaces.

Pamela Colman-Smith, nicknamed "Pixie," was a very cute, half-American, half-Jamaican woman, who was raised in England. She was a lesbian and an early feminist who became involved in the suffragette movement. Above all, she was a visionary artist who is best remembered as the illustrator of the Rider-Waite Tarot, though she received no acknowledgment or credit for it until 1938, when literary historians began to write about her.

Coleman-Smith spent much of her childhood between Jamaica and Britain, and went on to study art in New York as a young adult. Much of her early creative work, including writing and illustrating books, was centred on Jamaican folklore. You've probably encountered the artwork of Pamela Colman Smith before, even if you didn't realise that Colman-Smith drew the images for the most well-known tarot deck. These images have become cultural archetypes that are still commonly reprinted and used today.

Under her nickname Pixie, she was an active part of Irish poet William Butler Yeats' literary circle. She and Irish artist Jack B. Yeats co-published the literary magazine 'The Broad Sheet.' Colman-Smith eventually decided she wanted her own journal, however, and began 'The Green Sheaf.'

The Green Sheaf had 13 total issues, each printed on handmade paper and featuring hand-colored illustrations by Colman-Smith and other artists. The publication is sprinkled

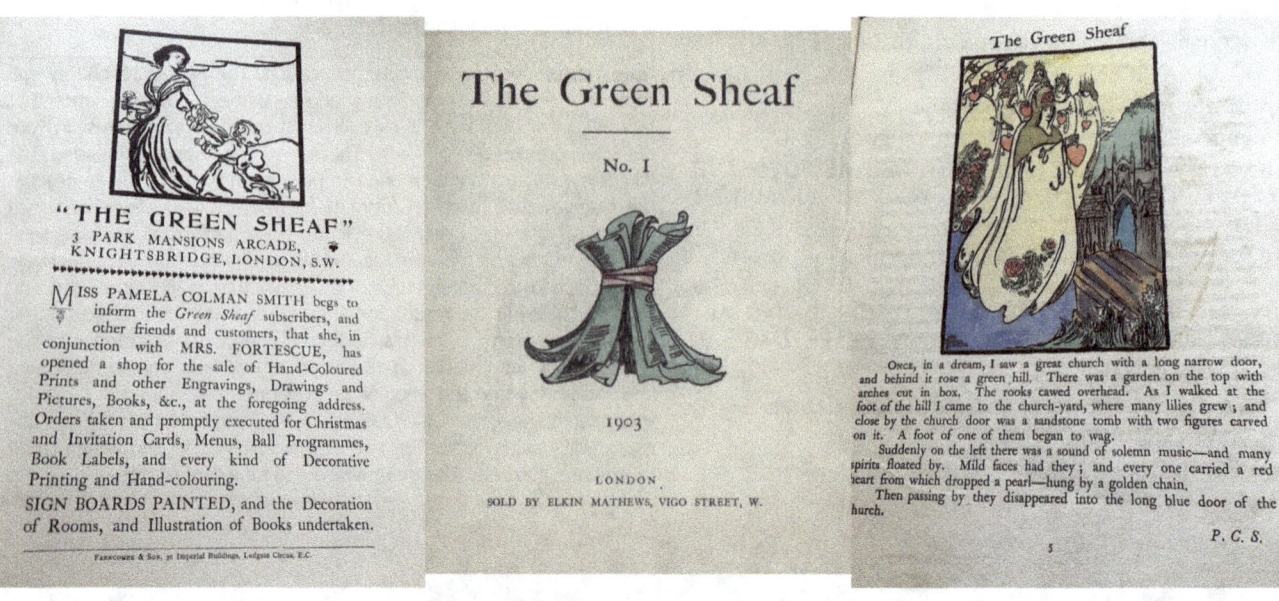

Green Sheaf No. 1 by Pamela Colman Smith (ed.), John J. Burns Library, Boston College.

with the works of well-known authors; George William Russell, Lady Gregory, William Blake and W.B. Yeats. The Green Sheaf is certainly a publication of magickal interest. It contained myths, spells and beautifully printed poetry and artwork.

ColmanSmith published books for other authors and offered custom orders for books. In addition to being an author, editor, publisher and bookseller, Colman-Smith also sold prints of her original artwork. Coleman-Smith opened a School of Hand-Colouring in 1904 in Knightsbridge, London.

Colman Smith was also a graphic designer whose creations were as diverse as lace work patterns, programs and advertising cards, bookplates, private Christmas cards, through to set designs for major play productions. Colman-Smith was also a stage performer. Under the pseudonym Gelukiezanger, Colman-Smith would dress in character to tell "West Indian Folk Stories." She later published these stories as "The Annancy Stories," (1899) that inspired Neil Gammon's "American Gods.".

One of Colman-Smith's Wartime poster designs | Pamela Colman-Smith performing as: "Gelukiezanger" | the facing plate of her book Annancy Stories

Pamela Colman-Smith Not Credited For The Ryder-Wait Deck.
Arthur Edward Wait together with Pamela Colman-Smith, created the world's most popular tarot deck. But if you hadn't previously heard of Pamela Colman Smith, you're not alone. Coleman-Smith's story sometimes gets missed out of tarot histories, and her name was left off of most editions of her tarot deck until recently

By the time that Wait ask Coleman-Smith for help with his tarot deck, she was already far more successful than he. She was already a well known author in her own right. She was indeed a highly sought after illustrator for children's books and governmental war posters. Additionally she worked for the literati of her day. People such as the poet William Butler Yeats, Bram Stocker, whom she called "Uncle Bramy," commissioned her to illustrate their work.

Waite never acknowledged the importance of Coleman-Smith's work. In the book written to accompany the cards, he failed to mention her by name, saying only that a "young black woman, a most imaginative and abnormally psychic artist," had illustrated the deck upon his instructions. This dismissive attitude is inexcusable as they were equal members of the same fraternal magickal order since 1901. Pamela had been a full member of 'The Order of the Golden Dawn' right along with the better known members such as William Butler Yeats, Florence Farr. She was a founding member of the Golden Dawn before Arthur Waite caused his faction. Coleman-Smith originally met Waite through the 'Hermetic Order of the Golden Dawn' occult organisation, in which they were both members.

Why would Waite always down played Coleman-Smith's contributions? And what reason could Waite have for going so far as to later dismiss this deck as his own creation?

Many tarot historians believe that the lion's share of the credit for the deck actually belongs to Coleman-Smith for the artwork and the authorship too. Waite later admitted in an interview that he only carefully controlled the creation of three cards: *"I saw to it that Pamela Coleman-Smith should not be picking up casually any floating images from my own or another mind. She had to be spoon-fed carefully over the Priestess card, over that which is called the Fool and over the Hanged Man."* In contradiction to this, letters survive in which Waite sends Coleman-Smith to the British museum to make sketches from the Italian 'Sola Busca Tarot' and asks for her interpretation of their meanings. The sketches are almost identical to the original Sola Busca. it being the first tarot to have illustrations on every card, where the preceding 'Marseilles Decks' only have numerical features on the suits.

Many people believed that Coleman-Smith wasn't paid for her work. Payment invalidates all successive copyright claims as it is a job rather than being a risk-taking contributor. This is apparently not true. According to an interview with Mr. Kaplan of US Games, *"Pamela Colman Smith sent* [a letter to] *Alfred Stieglitz in 1909 or 1910 telling him that she had just done a big job of 78 illustrations for very little money. That was the Rider-Waite Tarot deck."* A work for hire is a work created for another person for which you are paid in exchange for relinquishing claim on any rights to the work. If Coleman-Smith had not been paid, it would possibly call into question the chain of copyright ownership of the Rider-Waite Tarot in Europe. Since she was paid (even if it was 'very little'), she and her heirs had no further claim on the cards. However, int he absence of an exclusive contract, she was within her rights to resell the art and her other contributions.

De Laurence's "Square Yellow" tarot deck with Coleman-Smith artwork, first appeared in 1916, just 6 years after the release of The Rider Waite Deck. However, it has been speculated that the uncredited book "The Key to the Tarot," aka "Oracles Behind the Veil," that later accompanied the de Laurence Coleman-Smith Deck, was Pixie's original unedited notes to Waite on her studies of the 'Sola Busca Tarot' and her interpretation of their meanings. Pamela Coleman-Smith, was in the habit of reselling her work and making hand coloured prints of it. Coleman-Smith, who was orphaned and who could not receive her inheritance from her uncle until 1919, had to support herself. It is therefor very probable that she resold her illustration rights and notes to de Laurence. So why not put her name on it then? It should be remembered that the art work was a direct copy of a museum piece that was privately owned and therefore, could be legally encumbered by copyright issues.

Ecclesia Gnostica Catholica
Pamela converted to what she called esoteric Catholicism soon after illustrating the deck. There's no clear indication about what kind of Catholicism she converted to. However it is unlikely that traditional Catholicism was her choice. She was very interested in, and drawn to ritual in all its different incarnations. She grew up as a Swedenborgian. Her maternal grandfather was the first to publish the Swedenborgian papers in the States, and her family was involved in that church, which was very large in New York and England, especially in Manchester. She became aware of Obeah, whilst growing up in Jamaica and it was important to her. She says in an interview from around 1911 that "...the first time I went to Ireland is when I first saw fairies and pixies, and became aware of Celtic spiritualism." She was interested in religious structure, but not in a dogmatic way.

After the end of the First World War, Smith received an inheritance from an uncle that enabled her to buy a house in Bude, Cornwall, in an area popular with artists and bohemians. For income, she established a vacation/retirement home, very similar in type to Netherwood, for Catholic priests in a neighbouring house.

It is most likely that what Colman-Smith converted to, in 1911, was the Ecclesia Gnostica Catholica. The Ecclesia Gnostica Catholica (E.G.C.), or the Gnostic Catholic Church, is a Gnostic church organisation. It is the ecclesiastical arm of the Ordo Templi Orientis (O.T.O.), an international fraternal initiatory organisation devoted to promulgating the Law of Thelema, the catechism of Aleister Crowley. She had corresponded with Crowley after she became disillusioned with Arthur Wait and his Golden Dawn schism. Colman-Smith's boarding house for priests, fits into the style of the Profess-Houses of Crowley's Ordo Templi Orientis. One of his central goals for the Order was the establishment of Profess-Houses, which he also referred to as Retreats or Collegium ad Spiritum Sanctum. In the O.T.O. Manifesto, it is claimed that their exact location would be secret, known only to those who are entitled to use them but that they can be open to non-members. Among other things a Profess-House is for the purpose of being:

- A place where "members may conceal themselves in order to pursue the Great Work without hindrance"
- "They are also temples of true worship, specially consecrated by Nature to bring out of a man all that is best in him."
- "These houses are secret fortresses of Truth, Light, Power and Love"
- "Dignity and etiquette are to be strictly observed"
- "Brethren of advanced years and known merit" may retire at a Profess House.
- In his writings before his death/disappearance, Profess-Houses seemed to be of far greater value to Crowley than local bodies.

This certainly seems to be the kind of establishment that Pamela Colman-Smith was running. Bude is only a few miles from the Clovelly Church yard that appears to be the true final resting place of the remains of Alister Crowley. It is quite possible then that Crowley faked his death for a 2nd time and retired to this Profess House run by Coleman-Smith. (See article in previous issue)

Pamela Colman-Smith's Legacy

Colman-Smith's art work has become subconscious symbolism in the awareness of every modern spiritual person. It is inescapable. This makes her one of the most successful artists of all time. Artistically and personally was ahead of the time. She was an attractive woman who was very successful in business and society. She was one of the first people to identify herself as a graphic designer. She simultaneously made people embrace her racial identity and kept people guessing about it. For example, when she first met William Butler's father, he thought that she was Japanese. Even though she was with her father, who was white and from a very well known Brooklyn family, Pamela drew a caricature of herself as a woman in a kimono and gave it to Yeats. She embodied a fluid, non-binary identity. She was never married, she was never in any longterm relationship with a man. She lived with her partner, Nora Lake, for more than 20 years till her death. She was very focused on female-identified communities and spaces. Most of the people she interacted with, were women, many of whom self-identified as lesbian. But she never had any children of her own.

In her later life, the Profess-House in Bude continued to be her main occupation till her death. She became very reclusive. She never married, and she herself died in Bude, Cornwall on 18 September 1951. This is where she lived out her days, with the woman she loved, in the company of great spiritual minds and revolutionary hearts, like her own.

© Shé D'Montford 2020

MISS PAMELA COLEMAN SMITH

MISS COLMAN SMITH

IMAGE CREDIT
Imre Zsido. See more on page 36

ISRAEL REGARDIE
INITIATION & PSYCHOTHERAPY

The Hermetic Order of the Golden Dawn and the Ordo Rosae Rubeae et Aureae Crucis (R.R. et A.C.) are two divisions of an initiatic and magical Order founded by high-ranking Freemasons in England, respectively in 1888 and 1892. Although the exact origins of the Order remain obscure as well as controversial, its primary historical importance lies in its brilliant synthesis of mythical and magical material, from such varied sources as the Fama Fraternitatis (the first published Rosicrucian document), The Egyptian Book of the Dead, Cornelius Agrippa, Tycho Brahe, and John Dee. Salient aspects of the vast corpus of the Order's initiatic and magical material were first revealed in 1937 by the late Dr. Israel Regardie. This material has subsequently impacted most areas of modern magic, as well as many other arenas of spirituality.

Israel Regardie (1907-1985) stands as an important generational link to the magical rebirth of the late nineteenth century, as well as a pioneer in an early attempt to integrate psychology and magic. Born in 1907, Regardie as a young man knew both Aleister Crowley (1875-1947) and Dion Fortune (1890-1946), two early adepts of the Ordo Rosae Rubeae et Aureae Crucis, each of whom went on to found their own esoteric fraternities. Regardie was also initiated into the Stella Matutina, an early offshoot of the Golden Dawn. Finally, Regardie's work was groundbreaking as an early attempt to integrate psychology and magic.

When Regardie was a young man, he fervently wished to become a magician. He considered Aleister Crowley to be the foremost magician of the period and, having introduced himself to Crowley by means of an admiring letter, began to work as his personal secretary in Paris in 1928. After several years with Crowley, Regardie was forced to leave as the result of a painful rupture with his mentor. The trauma caused by this breach wounded Regardie deeply; he later said it took him nearly seven years to recover from it.

Impoverished and confused, Regardie was taken in as a house guest of Dion Fortune, who was living near Glastonbury in southwest England. Fortune was not only a talented magician but a natural clairvoyant as well. Until he died he never forgot her hospitality and generosity during this difficult period.

Dion Fortune influenced Regardie in a completely unexpected direction. She had been instrumental in bringing Sigmund Freud's ideas to England and had written a collection of short stories called The Secrets of Dr. Taverner. Although she characterized these stories as fiction, she said that Dr. Taverner actually existed and that the stories reflected factual case studies in which psychological and magical processes were linked.

It was at Dion Fortune's dinner table that Regardie was first exposed to the ideas of Freud and C. G. Jung. Shortly thereafter, still struggling with the onslaught of emotions stemming from his breach with Crowley, Regardie entered first into Freudian psychoanalysis and later into Jungian analysis. During this phase Regardie became aware of how great a role his own unresolved emotional conflicts from early childhood had played in his rupture with Crowley. Regardie eventually concluded that it was such unresolved infantility that accounted for most of the chaotic group dynamics of earlier esoteric fraternities. This would lead him to insist on the necessity of psychotherapy for anyone seriously practicing any spiritual discipline.

Regardie later moved to the U.S., where he became familiar with the ideas of Wilhelm Reich and entered into Reichian therapy. He also began to correspond with Reich's daughter Eva, which stimulated him to take a serious interest in the mind-body connection and at length to train as a chiropractor.

Even toward the end of his life, Regardie continued to respect both Freudian psychoanalysis and the ideas of Jung. He eventually came to believe, however, that Jungian analysis as he had experienced it was lacking in effective technique. He ultimately concluded that verbal therapy of any orientation paled in the light of Reich's bodywork, and that the techniques of ceremonial magic would one day become a powerful adjunct to psychotherapy.

As a therapist and a bodyworker, Regardie combined Reich's approach with minor chiropractic adjustments, basic magical techniques, and hatha yoga. In a typical session, Regardie would begin by initiating deep, rhythmic breathing in the client for a considerable period of time. This hyperventilation would create a slightly altered state of consciousness. During this process Regardie would survey various areas of tension on the body and would reduce their tightness with a type of deep and at times painful massage.

Both Regardie and Reich felt that unresolved emotional conflicts were stored in the body as tension. Using a physical approach would release blockages so that life energy, which Reich called "orgone," could pass freely through the entire body. During the course of a session, a great deal of emotion would frequently emerge, which the client was encouraged to express.

Regardie often related Reichian ideas to the magic of the Hermetic Order of the Golden Dawn. He was particularly fond of one magical exercise called the Middle Pillar Ritual. In this technique the magician visualizes successive spheres of light at various points above, below, and along the spinal column while vibrating certain words. This generates a certain kind of energy, which, according to Regardie, is identical to Reich's orgone. This energy is then circulated around and through the entire body by means of further visualization.

Legitimate esoteric orders have always been primarily intended to provide a context within which initiation may safely and effectively occur. As will be shown here, there are many parallels between initiation and forms of psychotherapy that take into account the spiritual dimensions of growth. Regardie even advised that the two should be considered as complementary processes, and that initiation should always be accompanied by some form of psychotherapy.

Regardie of course considered Reichian therapy to be the most useful adjunct to magical work. In view of the current lack of trained Reichian therapists, however, other schools of psychology suitable for work alongside magical training are those that include spiritual growth as a part of their paradigm, such as the Jungian and Transpersonal orientations, Psychosynthesis, and the emerging school of Esoteric Psychology.

Why does a candidate for initiation need psychotherapy? Any form of spiritual training, when practiced with enough sincerity and discipline, will eventually activate what Jung calls the complexes of the personal unconscious. These may be defined as infantile emotional patterns left over from very early childhood that revolve around unresolved parental conflicts. These complexes are symbolized in the digrams in this appendix by the seven-headed dragon. Frequently they are energized by spiritual practices.

Unless the complexes are allowed to emerge into consciousness in a safe and controlled fashion, they can be acted out in dangerous ways. This helps explain why many "spiritual" groups have become dysfunctional and at times even destructive.

Admittedly, combining initiation and psychotherapy does involve some difficulties. Whereas psychotherapy is unlikely to harm the effectiveness of an initiation or of any other genuinely spiritual process, not everyone seeking initiation can afford the substantial expense of psychotherapy. Furthermore the average lay person may find it difficult to distinguish an effective therapist from an incompetent one. Unfortunately, inept and destructive psychotherapists are frequently easier to find than capable ones, and the same holds true for initiators and initiating orders. Far too many esoteric groups are primarily motivated by their leaders' needs for money or manipulative control over people's lives.

True initiation is a process not unlike that of psychotherapy in that the skill and personal ethics of the initiator are crucial to a successful outcome. Moreover a relationship with an unethical initiator can be as damaging as one with an unethical psychotherapist. Anyone seeking initiation thus needs to be extremely discriminating in the choice of an initiator or order.

The seeker also needs to distinguish between initiating orders and personality cults, since far too many spiritual groups have been built around the personalities of charismatic but manipulative leaders. This phenomenon, combined with a disregard for the psychological issues that may arise, accounts for many of the abuses that have plagued the esoteric community.

An analysis of the psychological dynamics underlying initiation will help to clarify why such abuses occur. The initiatic process of the Hermetic Order of the Golden Dawn clearly illustrates the dangers as well as the potential of initiation. But let us first consider the primary differences between initiation and psychotherapy.

Initiation, as its name suggests, may be defined as a new beginning. In the Golden Dawn system, the initiatic process has a magical as well as a psychological component. The magical component may be described as the systematic awakening or ignition of certain forces or energies in the "Sphere of Sensation" of the initiate. (The Sphere of Sensation is the term used by the Ordo Rosae Rubeae et Aureae Crucis to describe what is commonly called the energy body or the aura.)

This process requires an initiator in whom these forces are already awakened and active, since initiation occurs through an actual transmission of energies. Thus from a magical perspective, the relationship between the initiator and the candidate is crucial. In this sense genuine self-initiation, if not altogether impossible, is at least extremely difficult to achieve. It is nonetheless possible, although difficult, to accomplish much of this magical aim of initiation through systematically and repeatedly invoking the correct magical energies using ceremonial magic

Although much has been written about the Hermetic Order of the Golden Dawn. almost nothing has been said about the overall initiatic process in which the Golden Dawn is but the first step. From the beginning, this system was conceived as being composed ten grades, each one corresponding to a Sephirah on the Qabalistic Tree of Life, and of three degrees, each one corresponding to an entire order. Each successive order is veiled from the previous one by the veils of Isis and Nephthys (called Paroketh).

The first degree and order consist of the curriculum and cycle of initiations of the Hermetic Order of the Golden Dawn. The grades of the first degree begin with the Neophyte initiation and correspond to the Sephiroth of Malkuth, Yesod, Hod, and Netsach. The second degree and order are those of the Ordo Rosae Rubeae et Aureae Crucis. The Grades of the second degree begin with the probationary

The Three Orders on the Tree of Life

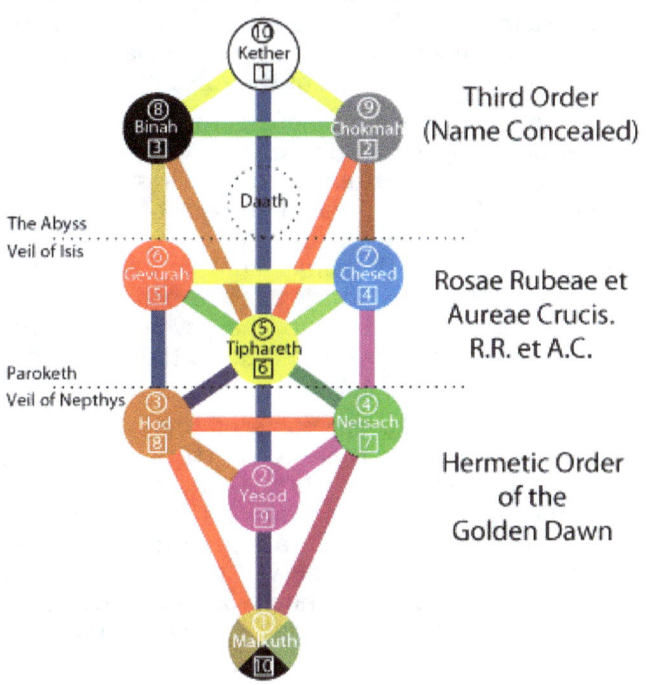

Third Order (Name Concealed)

Rosae Rubeae et Aureae Crucis. R.R. et A.C.

Hermetic Order of the Golden Dawn

initiation of the Portal of the Vault of the Adepti and correspond to the Sephiroth of Tiphareth, Gevurah, and Chesed. The third degree and order are those of the Third Order, whose true name remains concealed. The grades of the third order correspond to the Sephiroth of Binah, Chokmah, and Kether, and begin with the probationary initiation of the Portal of the Abyss (which corresponds to Non-Sephirah of Daath).

In the first order, the magical forces are awakened, activated, and balanced in the candidate by the initiator in the rituals themselves. These forces are those of the traditional elements; Fire, Water, Air, Earth, and Spirit, which are symbolized by a pentagram. Beginning in the second order, however, the individual practice of ceremonial magic greatly enhances this process. The Second Order work primarily activates the forces of the seven traditional planets: Saturn, Jupiter, Mars, the Sun, Venus, Mercury, and the Moon, which are symbolized by a hexagram. Furthermore, in the second order, the adept learns to independently work with the elements through a series of sub-grades, which further differentiates these forces in the adept's aura. The third order primarily activates the forces of the signs of the zodiac, as well as alchemical Salt, Sulfur, and Mercury, which are symbolized by a triangle. Thus the work of the third order includes alchemy as a psycho-spiritual process as well as ceremonial magic.

Having thus examined the magical aspect of initiation, we may now understand the significance of the symbol of the Rose Cross (shown here) used by the Ordo Rosae Rubeae et Aureae Crucis. Though its imagery is too intricate to be fully discussed here, we might point out that this Rose Cross symbolically depicts the forces awakened in the energy body of a fully initiated adept. It also illustrates the harmony and equilibrium of their operation, as represented by the four elements, the seven traditional planets, and the twenty-two petals of the rose.

The three concentric rings of Hebrew letters in the center of the figure are divided into groups of three, seven, and twelve letters each. This distribution is taken from the Sefer Yetzirah or "Book of Formation" of the ancient Qabalists. The innermost ring corresponds to the first order and the forces of the elements. The second ring corresponds to the second order as well as to the seven traditional planets, while the third correlates to the third order and the signs of the Zodiac.

Let us go on to examine some of the dynamics of psychotherapy in order to better understand initiation from a psychological perspective. According to certain schools of psychology, a phenomenon called "transference" figures prominently in effective psychotherapy. Transference may be defined as the process of becoming conscious of our unresolved parental conflicts. During the course of psychotherapy, the client begins to see the therapist as embodying these unresolved conflicts. This occurs as the client projects the contents of his or her own unconscious onto the therapist in much the same fashion as a film is projected onto a blank screen.

Transference also plays a crucial role in the process of initiation, except that here it is the initiator who becomes the screen for the projections. This is one reason why initiation may be such an extremely effective tool in facilitating personal as well as spiritual development. But it also explains why initiation in the hands of inept or unscrupulous leaders can lead to heartbreak, disappointment, or even death and destruction. Moreover, because the transferential relationship with another human being is a central factor in initiation as well, genuine self-initiation is as impossible as self-administered psychotherapy.

As we have already mentioned, psychotherapy concurrent with initiation is a good idea, even if it is not always possible. But certain special circumstances do need to be considered. Certainly the therapist should be able to regard spirituality as a healthy phenomenon; ideally he or she should have experience working with spiritual issues.

Although the therapist and the initiator do not need to consult each other, they must maintain healthy boundaries in their relationship with the initiate. It is never a good idea for a therapist to discuss case material outside the therapeutic relationship. Unfortunately some therapists tend to discuss this material with colleagues, supervisors, even sometimes at cocktail parties, all the while believing that they are behaving ethically because they only use the client's first name.

Both the therapist and the initiator need to understand from the outset that such discussions must not occur. Initiation may be likened to an alchemical process: in order to be most effective, the vessel - the relationships with therapist and initiator - needs to be hermetically sealed. This is the primary reason that such great importance is given to secrecy and silence in esoteric matters. Silence creates power and pressure, which ultimately produce profound spiritual and psychological transformation.

Whether the primary transference occurs with the initiator or the therapist is relatively unimportant. One never consciously decides to create a transferential relationship. It happens completely unconsciously, taking place with the person one is most able to fall in both love and hate with. What matters most is that it occur and that the negative projections and feelings be allowed to emerge and be safely worked through.

The earliest phase of the initiatic process of the first degree is symbolically depicted in a diagram called

Figure 1

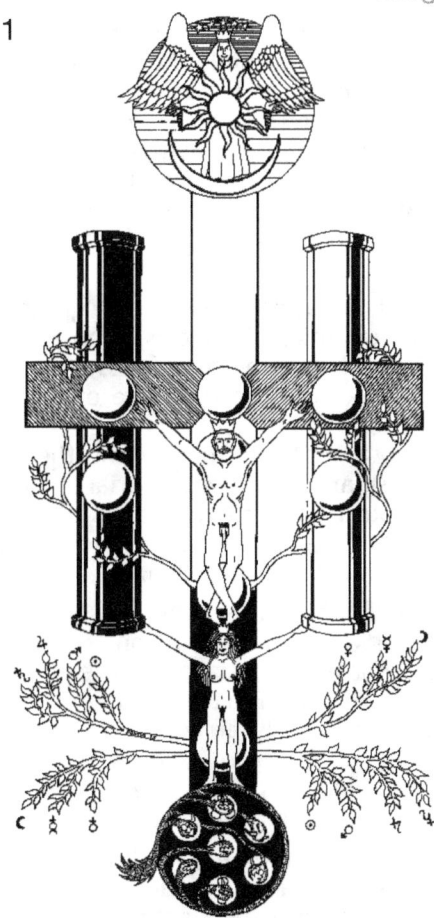

"The Garden of Eden before the Fall" (figure 1). This diagram, which is presented to the initiate in the 3=8 grade of Practicus, represents a stage of primordial innocence. At this stage the candidate typically sees the initiator in an unrealistically positive light as a sort of ideal or perfect parent. In this diagram, Eve, the female figure shown at the bottom of the Tree of Life, represents the ideal mother (and the Qabalistic nephesh or instinctual nature); she is depicted supporting the pillars of Jachin and Boaz. Adam, representing the ideal father (and the Qabalistic ruach or the rational aspect) stands above her with his chest at the station of Tiphareth, arms outstretched towards Chesed and Gevurah.

This diagram represents the bliss of innocence: the candidate is living in a state of bliss because of his or her contact with the "ideal parents" as projected onto the initiator. This process is not unlike Jung's portrayal of falling in love. According to Jung, when men fall in love, they project their own feminine side or anima onto the beloved, while women project the inner masculine, which Jung calls the animus.

This is the stage that is most susceptible to abuse by inept or unscrupulous initiators. Allegations of sexual harassment, manipulation, and other forms of abuse have surfaced, not merely surrounding leaders of occult orders, but in the mainstream religious community as well. As Jim Jones, David Koresh, and the Order of the Solar Temple have proven, this abuse of trust may even have fatal consequences.

Certain safeguards, such as laws enforcing ethical guidelines, have been set up for psychotherapy. But as yet there are no such laws protecting initiates in esoteric fraternities, though emotional, physical, or sexual abuse in these areas can be just as damaging. The decision to enter initiation may therefore be likened to the decision to enter psychotherapy, and the choice of a suitable initiator is at least as important as that of a good psychotherapist. In both choices individuals should be extremely judicious.

A further examination of the diagram of "The Garden of Eden before the Fall" reveals the illusory nature of the relationship with the ideal parents. One notices first of all the absence of the Supernal Sephiroth (Kether, Binah, and Chokmah) on this Qabalistic Tree of Life: they are symbolized only in potential by the winged female figure at the top of the Tree. This figure symbolizes the neshamah, or Divine Feminine, of the Qabalists. Furthermore Eve (the female figure at the foot of the Tree) stands upon a coiled seven-headed dragon.

This dragon has a long history. It is to be found as early as the Paleolithic period in the form of the serpent associated with the consort of the Great Mother Goddesses as well as with her Tree of Life. This same serpent appears later in the Egyptian myths of Ra's struggles with the serpent-fiend Apep. In this same negative light it is encountered yet again in the New Testament book of Revelation.

Nonetheless the serpent remains an important symbol of resurrection and the renewal of life, since it sheds its skin on a regular basis. When interpreted psychologically, this serpentine dragon represents what Jung calls the complexes of the personal unconscious.

The unfolding initiatic process inevitably leads to the situation represented by the diagram entitled "The Garden of Eden after the Fall" (Figure 2). This diagram is shown to the candidate during initiation

Figure 2

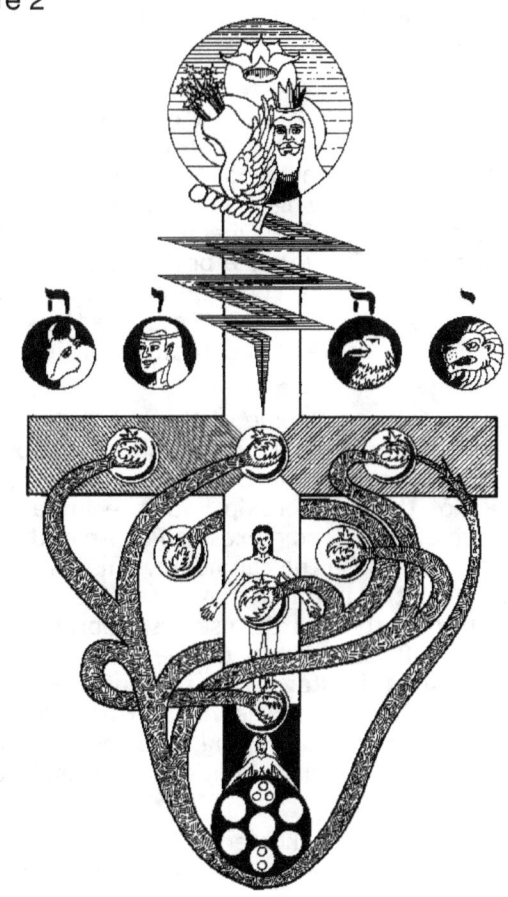

Figure 3

into the 4=7 grade of Philosophus. Here the heads of the dragon arise into consciousness; as shown in the diagram, they attach themselves to the seven lower Sephiroth on the Tree of Life. At this phase the initiate's ego is assaulted by his or her personal complexes. This is a necessary process for the awakening psyche, but it tends to be an unpleasant one.

How many love affairs have ended in disappointment or tragedy? Both the psychotherapeutic and initiatic processes further expose the unresolved conflicts of early childhood. The beloved, who once was seen in an imaginarily positive light, now becomes invested in the opposite fashion. The Queen of Heaven becomes the Hag, and the Fairy Prince becomes the Ogre. The same person who once "could do no wrong" suddenly "can do no right." These negative projections are, of course, as unrealistic as the positive projections of the previous phase.

It is crucial to the outcome of the initiation that the complexes of the personal unconscious be allowed to manifest in a safe and controlled way within the container of the relationship with the initiator. The emergence of these complexes can cause outbursts of irrational behavior in the candidate. This can be quite traumatic for the initiator as well as the candidate, as both frequently find themselves embroiled in the unresolved infantile drama of the candidate's early childhood. At this stage the skill of the initiator becomes crucial. He or she needs to be extremely conscious of what is happening, and sometimes must have almost superhuman patience to endure the candidate's outbursts.

This situation is complicated by what psychologists call "countertransference," in which the initiator's own personal complexes are projected onto the candidate. Initiators and therapists should never assume that they have become completely conscious of their own inner processes; no matter how much one has grown, one is always vulnerable to the further emergence of one's own unconscious material. The initiator may even erupt into outbursts of irrational behavior, which may further escalate the situation.

This phase of initiation is also fertile ground for abuse by inept or unethical initiators, who may either be blinded by their own complexes or tempted to maintain the positive transference of the first stage. The adoration of students can easily seduce an initiator into attempting to maintain the illusory role of the charismatic, idealized patriarch or matriarch. But this would be poison to successful initiation and spiritual growth as well as to the health of any legitimate spiritual organization.

Initiators must therefore resist this tendency at all costs; otherwise the initiation cannot progress beyond the phase symbolized by "The Garden of Eden before the Fall." Furthermore, the negative transference inevitably arrives! If a leader is unable or unwilling to become a focal point for these unpleasant projections, he or she will find some other object for them to be projected onto.

This leads to extremely unhealthy situations. Unscrupulous leaders are frequently obliged to find or create one or more scapegoats to serve as objects of the negative projections. This can lead to a pattern of abuse within, and expulsion from, the group. In the worst cases it leads to growing paranoia, as the scapegoat is projected onto an imaginary enemy or

Figure 4

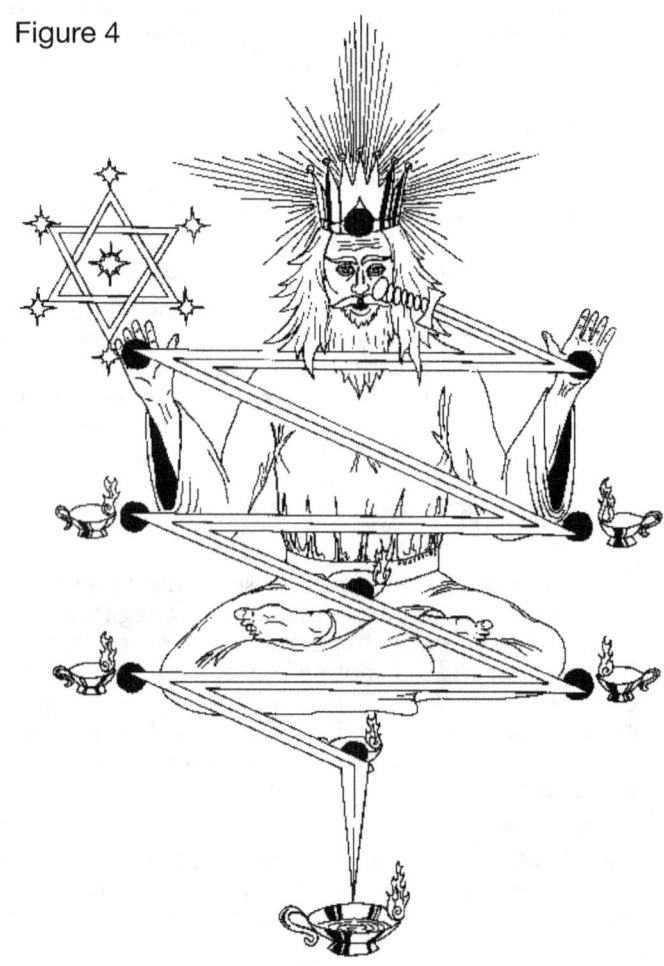

even society at large. Waco, Texas and Cheiry, Switzerland have become monuments to the danger of this dynamic.

At this point the esoteric community has placed far too little emphasis on personal growth and group dynamics. Yet it must be remembered that any time one comes into contact with spiritual energies, the contents of the personal unconscious will become activated as well. Hence esoteric orders need to facilitate personal growth alongside spiritual growth. The dynamics of personal interactions within these groups needs to be examined as well.

Throughout the first degree, the candidate was gradually entering into an entirely new relationship with his or her own Higher Self. In the early stages of the initiation, this relationship manifested chiefly through the unconscious projections onto the initiator. In the Portal Ritual of the Hermetic Order of the Golden Dawn, the seeds were planted to enable the relationship of the candidate with the Higher Self to become fully conscious. This birth into consciousness then occurs with the entry into the Ordo Rosae Rubeae et Aureae Crucis during the initiation into the 5=6 grade of Adeptus Minor.

In the early part of this ritual, the candidate is symbolically bound to a cross (which symbolizes the elements). This voluntary subordination of the ego to the Higher Self at length liberates the ego from the onslaught of the unconscious complexes. This is symbolized by the dropping away of the heads of the dragon from the Sephiroth (Figure 3).

After this stage of the ritual, the candidate is brought inside the Vault of the Adepti for the first time. This vault, a highly charged magical chamber, is the symbolic burial place of Christian Rosenkreutz (Frater CRC). As a place where the initiate is reborn, the vault thus partakes not only of the symbolism of tomb but that of the womb as well.

Once inside the vault the candidate is led to the head of the Pastos, the symbolic sarcophagus of Christian Rosenkreutz. When the lid of the Pastos is eventually removed to reveal the hidden figure of the Chief Adept (the initiator) inside, the candidate symbolically becomes illuminated by an influx of consciousness coming from the Higher Self. The new adept thus begins to enter into an entirely new and fully conscious relationship with this Higher Self (Figure 4).

During this investigation we have gained an understanding of the psychological as well as the magical processes underlying legitimate initiation. This, however, is not the end. Many years ago Regardie called for further exploration of the integration of psychology and magic. In fact, one might call the area of overlap between these two fields "Esoteric Psychology." This inquiry has been an attempt to make a small contribution to this emerging new field. The work, however, is just beginning. Standing at the vantage point of the end of the millennium, ten years after Regardie's death, we feel obliged to repeat his appeal for further research: "Whoever does succeed in welding these two [psychology and magic] indissolubly together, to him mankind will ever be grateful."

Copyright © 1995 Cris Monnastre & David Griffin

David Griffin is Rosicrucian Imperator at Hermetic Order of the Golden Dawn is S.L. MacGregor Mathers' present sucessor as Imperator of the Alpha Omega Rosicrucian Mystery School & the Hermetic Order of the Golden Dawn. David is today charged with the mission to train Magicians in the ancient Hermetic Mysteries of Solar Ascension. Griffin is also an independent Christian Bishop holding multiple lines of apostolic succession, a high grade Freemason (33, 90, 96 Degree - Ancient & Primitive Rite of Memphis-Mizraim- in possession of the complete & true Arcana Arcanorum, 32 AASR, KT, IX Swedish Rite), & an initiate of several other Continental European Rosicrucian & Hermetic societies whose names remain secret. David additionally holds Martinist esoteric transmissions as well os those of the Gold und Rosenkreutz Order, the Asiatic Brethren (Fratres Lucis), the Frères Ainées de la Rose Croix (F.A.R.+C.) & several other European Rosicrucian & Hermetic orders & societies. Griffin holds substantial additional Rosicrucian initiatic transmissions. These include the Gold und Rosenkreutz Order, the Asiatic Brethren, the Societas Rosicruciana of Backstrom, Reaux Croix, & the Rose Cross of Egypt (Rose Croix d'Orient). From 1992-1994, Cris Monnastre regularly initiated & advanced David Griffin into each of the Grades of the Hermetic Order of the Golden Dawn at the Alpha et Omega II temple in Los Angeles, then into the Portal & Adeptus Minor grades of the R.R. et A.C. David Griffin's is the author of The Ritual Magic Manual (Golden Dawn Publishing: 1999), in which Griffin finished the integration begun by S.L. MacGregor Mathers of the Qabalistic & Enochian systems for the elemental & astrological magic of the Golden Dawn.n 2002, David Griffin met in Paris with Frater L.E.T., representing the same Continental European order of Hermetic alchemists who had initiated Kenneth MacKenzie, to whom S.L. MacGregor Mathers referred to as the "Secret Chiefs." Griffin received the same Hermetic and Rosicrucian lineages transmitted earlier to MacKenzie by Count Apponyi and to Mathers by Lux E Tenebris, as well as an esoteric corpus and skeletal initiation rituals with which to create the "Third Order" that had since its inception been intended to complete the "three order" system of the Golden Dawn.

In 1994, **Cris Monnastre** was involved in a Golden Dawn schism. Griffin sided with Monnastre & became Imperator Ordinis of the Monnastre's Hermetic Order of the Golden Dawn. In 1998, Cris Monnastre retired from the Golden Dawn, leaving Griffin in charge. In 1999, Griffin was advanced through the 7=4 Grade of the Golden Dawn's Second Order (R.R. et A.C.) at the Ahathoor Temple No. 7 in Paris. The lineages descending from Desmond Bourke, Countess Bourkoun, and Marquis Tereschenko were transmitted to Griffin, who took the initiatic name of "Lux Ex Septentrionis" (Light From the North, which was the motto used by one of MacGregor Mathers' "Secret Chiefs" in Paris). Griffin's Golden Dawn order (formally Monnastre/Griffin's) was merged into the European headquartered, Hermetic Order of the Golden Dawn

The Art of Imre Zsido

● How do you describe your own art?
Surrealist-Fantasy Art with symbolistic imagery. This style of drawing for me is a subconscious process created by inspiration and imagination and inner obsession. The creative impetus leads me into an artistic mode with universal themes of unlimited fantasy and self-discovery. My unlimited desire to read books has ultimately transformed the painstaking process of creating my visionary images-specially the highly detailed ink drawings taking up to 300 hours – into another kind of world, a labor of love and spiritual nourishment.

● What inspires you?
I'm inspired by stories and books and also my internal imagery. My brand of surrealism is also inspired by the absurdity and excesses of human life. Some of my works are surely influenced by mythological and spiritual subjects and magic and mystery. I feel I'm connected to a timeless source of fantastic imagery and to my inner perceptions while transcribing lucid and waking dreams.

● What is your future aims and goals?
I love Art and would like to be a good artist, to improve my creative process with more self training and further learning of the different drawing and painting techniques... I think I also have to admit that I would love to work on book illustrations full time like a professional.

"..My works are surely influenced by mythological & spiritual subjects & magic & mystery…"

MAGICK

MAGICK MAGAZINE

THE ESOTERIC GARDEN

by Paul Goodall FRC

All of us, I am sure, if we are fortunate enough to have space for a garden, enjoy being close to our plants. Small or extravagantly large, each garden is a microcosm of hidden energies that on occasion we feel particularly in touch with. We can't put a finger on precisely the effect that our self-created bit of nature has on us, but when we feel physically tired or mentally drained, our gardens seem to have a magical ability to leave us calm in body and invigorated in thought. They are also havens of inspiration and many a poet and writer has benefited from their captivating spell. We might say that the 'Book of Nature' is a veritable text, full of divine meaning , if we know how to interpret its manifold pages.

From a Rosicrucian perspective we understand this in terms of the Universal Mind and pantheistic philosophy where God is seen as being and residing in everything in the material and immaterial realms. This can be complemented perhaps by the traditional belief in India that plants are in perpetual meditation and attuned to the primal mantra *Om*, which is breathed out by the Sun and sent to Earth. This is succinctly and beautifully summed up by Wolf-dieter Storl in his 2001 edition, Pflanzendevas (The Spiritual Nature of Plants):

> THE PRIMAL MANTRA, EMBODIED IN LIGHT, IS TRANSMITTED TO US BY PLANTS IN A LIFE-GIVING PROCESS. ONLY PLANTS ARE ABLE TO CONNECT IN THIS WAY THE CELESTIAL AND MUNDANE REALMS. IN THE SACRED LANGUAGE OF THE VEDAS PLANTS ARE DESIGNATED BY THE WORD OSADHI. THE WORD IS MADE UP OF OSA (BURNING TRANSFORMATION) AND DHI (VESSEL). IN THIS SENSE PLANTS CAN BE REGARDED AS VESSELS FOR THE METAMORPHOSIS OF THE COSMIC FIRE.[1]

This is a profound mystical viewpoint that sees plants at the centre of an alchemical process of life, as agents between the sun and us. While we might disagree with some of the metaphysical principles in this passage, as Rosicrucians we can certainly identify with the Cosmic essence being evoked.

Plant Alchemy

But returning to the quiet of our gardens, as we silently reflect on the greenery and life all around us, do we think of the vibratory energies manifesting and changing within it before our very eyes? Plants are continually working an internal alchemical process of transmutation; don't we just marvel at those time-lapse sequences in nature documentaries where we can observe their outer growth and transformation in such fascinating brevity and detail?

This inner alchemy is of course manifested in a very real chemical process called photosynthesis that is instigated by the photons of light generated by the sun. And this is where the Hindu viewpoint expressed in the quotation above contrasts, but also resonates in a deep spiritual way with real life science. Photosynthesis is the way a plant makes food for itself. The pigment chlorophyll in the "green" part of the leaves captures energy from the sun and this powers the building of food from very simple ingredients, carbon dioxide and water.

Water, containing valuable nutrients and minerals, is drawn out of the soil by the plant's roots and passed up through the leaves where they mix with carbon dioxide from the air and are converted into sugars that are absorbed by the plant to make it grow. During this process the plant releases oxygen, and together with the absorption of carbon dioxide, performs a vital function in maintaining the atmosphere of our planet.

The Elements

Taking stock of all the components in this energy cycle, we can see a working example of the interacting alchemical elements of Earth, Water, Air and Fire. Rudolf Steiner, the founder of the

Anthroposophical movement, saw the four elements reflected in the constituent parts of the plant as follows:

- Roots = Earth
- Leaves = Water
- Blossom = Air
- Seed = Fire

The use of the elements in Japanese Zen gardens is self-evident; being loaded with esoteric symbolism and havens of deliberate manipulation of plants, water, rocks and architectural features, together with the use of wind, fire and suchlike, to increase the atmosphere of spiritual tranquillity. in the West, we tend to be a bit more conservative and remain within traditional and national archetypal models of which there are quite a few. Not that there is anything wrong with that, of course; we get the most out of our gardens by remaining within our cultural parameters and the kinds we identify with in the West range from the cottage garden through to more formal arrangements. Ours tend to gravitate more toward the earth element with some emphasis on the watery side, whereas Japanese garden designs tend to combine all the elements in theirs.

Perhaps we also tend to work too much between a functional approach and one of aesthetic design where, for example, we want the patio to be large enough for a table, six chairs and a barbecue. In a small garden this might have a detrimental effect, being less conducive toward achieving a haven of peace and calm. A medium sized or large garden can have all the stops pulled out and there will be ample room to experiment. One can however combine functionality and beauty, even with some symbolic content. Read up on Japanese gardens to see what would be useful to you. They have much to offer.

Heavenly Cycles

The energy of a plant is never stationary, there is always change, whether in a daily, monthly or annual rhythm. The all-important cycle is of course the annual revolution of the earth around the sun, giving us our four seasons or spring , summer, autumn and winter. But there is also the

ancient tradition of lunar gardening where planting and harvesting is carried out according to the lunar cycle.

Passages in the works of Homer and Hesiod suggest that the Greeks used lunar months. In his *Works and Days*, Hesiod in the 8th Century BCE, showed that he often used the constellations to plan the planting and harvesting of crops. In more modern times this system died out because of the increased use of fertilisers; but in recent decades the practice has been revived, largely due to Steiner's biodynamic agricultural system that he developed in the 1920s.

Lunar Gardening

As we have been discussing lunar cycle based gardening, we might well ask, how does it work? There appear to be a combination of lunar effects such as the differing amounts of light reflected from the moon, its gravitational pull on plant fluids, the tidal effect on the water table and the distortions in the Earth's magnetic field.

Lunar gardeners believe the moon's gravitational pull affects the flow of moisture in the soil. This effect would be strongest at the new and full moon phases, when the sun and moon are approximately lined up with the earth. It is weakest at the first and last quarter moon phases. So, to take advantage of the lunar cycle, the gardener must avoid turning the soil when it contains the greatest amount of moisture during the new and full moon period when reflected solar light and the gravitational pull is the greatest. The elevated moisture content encourages seeds to sprout and grow, especially with the light of a full moon since this is thought to have an effect on seed germination.

One particular modern advocate of this method of gardening is Maria Thun, whose books on this subject have influenced gardeners and farmers throughout the world. There is now an abundant literature on the subject of gardening by the moon, and annual lunar calendars have become indispensable for many gardeners.

Practical Suggestions

There are several practical things we might do to help stay in touch with the natural world of our gardens. Concerning the moon and its effect, go out into the garden at night and just sit or stand still and quietly sense how the various energies are at work during the different phases of the lunar cycle. Try to empathise with how the plants are experiencing the moon's influence, and 'feel' if you can, how the plants respond to the moon's phases.

Gently hold the leaves or trunk and try to feel the vibrational energy within. Do it in daytime as well, picking up on the Cosmic essence of the sun, feeling the life that is being received by all you see. Breathe in this Cosmic influence and feel the plants doing the same. Try these exercises at different times of day; they are very beneficial and place you in deep attunement with the myriad life-forms around you in your small patch of greenery. As you attune yourself to the subtle patterns of ebb and flow, and cycles within cycles, you will deepen your rapport with the plants and insects in your garden.

But to get back to my opening musing on the beneficial effect that gardens give us. Our gardens are temporary environments allowing us some welcome respite from a world that seems at times the opposite of what we would expect from something so innately divine and wholly part of the Cosmic. during our time on Earth we encounter the bad or dark things in life as well as the good. This is unavoidable and is part and parcel of our progress towards self-knowledge.

But considering our garden plants, they have their roots in the darkness and shoots in the light, and their sustenance is gained from both worlds, above and below. We can learn from them that the path of our spiritual progress involves bringing these two metaphysical polarities of light and dark, sun and moon, together in ourselves in mutual harmony in our eternal quest to move closer to the God of our highest understanding.

1. English quotation from Christopher Mcintosh, Gardens of the Gods, I.B. Tauris, 2005, p.138.

Reprinted with permission from The Rosicrucian magazine. Paul Goodhall is a member of the Rosicrucian Order AMORC. Available as a digital download from www.amorc.org.au/rosicrucianbooks

PLUG INTO THE POWER OF THE UNIVERSE

For over 100 years, the Rosicrucian Order has made available its successful system of personal, home based study that gives you access to the fullest potential of being – physical, mental, psychic and spiritual. In simple weekly lessons you will find that our comprehensive approach makes your learning and personal development process easy.

We invite you to join with us and become part of a worldwide group of men and women dedicated to mystical knowledge in the widest sense.

You can harness virtually unlimited powers of insight, creativity, spirituality. You can attract people and events into your life, speed your body's natural healing processes, create harmony around you. And much more. All you have to do is learn how.

As the first step in discovering just how extraordinary you really are we invite you to read our free introductory booklet *MASTERY OF LIFE* - see it at: www.amorc.org.au or ask for your free no obligation copy by phoning: 1300 88 11 35 or email: mastery@amorc.org.au

AMORC — THE ROSICRUCIAN ORDER

THE ROSICRUCIAN ORDER IS NON-PROFIT, NON-RELIGIOUS, NON-POLITICAL

MAGICK

It is our aim to make this the best and most reliable resource for Magickal information internationally

Magick Magazine is a unique magazine for the magickal community

Its writers, artists, editors, marketing managers advertisers and production crew are all well respected members of the community.

There are no muggles or unethical people involved in this work.

The magazine will be posted on line in a flipbook format or you can order a full colour softcover book for $12.95 plus postage.

ADVERTISING RATES

Full Page		
A — Dimensions 277mm (H) x 190mm (W)		$800
Half Page		
B — Dimensions 135mm (H) x 190mm (W)		$400
Quarter Page		
C — Dimensions 135mm (H) x 93mm (W)		$200
One-eighth Page		
D — Dimensions 65mm (H) x 93mm (W)		$100
Banner Page		
E — Dimensions 30mm (H) x 190mm (W)		$120
Classied Display advert		
F — Dimensions 30mm (H) x 44.5mm (W)		$50
Classied Line advert		
G — 3 lines or 30 words.		$30

VIEW ONLINE AT http://www.magick.org.au

Conditions of advertising: All prices include artwork design

+61402 793 604

YOUTH SPELL OVER DONE

A 44-year-old witch is today suffering the effects of an overdone youth spell, after losing track of the time she spent in her cauldron of renewal.

We spoke to spellcraft expert, Mrs. Madge Ick, who said, "A youth spell is really very simple, you just have to mix up the ingredients in your cauldron, heat it to body temperature, then immerse yourself in the brew until you reach the desired age. The basic potion reverses age at about 1 year per minute, but you have to keep an eye on your progress with a mirror and a clock, as there can be some variation according to the strength of the brew, the heat of the water or the age of the user."

Apparently, the witch in question was using her mobile phone to time the spell, when she received a call from her distraught teenage daughter who had just broken up with her boyfriend. By the time she had calmed her daughter down, the witch had spent more than 35 minutes in the cauldron.

The daughter said, "I began to get the feeling something was wrong when mother started giggling and said it was good that I'd got rid of the yucky boy. I couldn't get any sense out of her after that, so I called the Spellcraft Home Intervention Team and we both arrived at the house about 5 minutes later and hauled her, kicking and screaming, out of the cauldron. She bit one of the emergency team because she wanted to stay and play in the water. She's just not Mum anymore – she can't even cackle now, she just giggles. The worst of it is, I'll have to look after her till she grows up. And honestly, she's a brat!"

YOUTH SPELL VICTIM AS FOUND BY EMERGENCY TEAM

Morganna with her warm humour is a well respected elder of our community. You can contact her on morganna13@hotmail.com

CASTING MAGICK BY POST

Praise Mercury; the swiftness of communication is at an all-time high in human civilisation. No more than a minute before typing this I sent an email to a friend in the Caribbean (hey Fiona Horne, love ya!), and another to a friend in the UK (hey Sshivani Durga, love ya too!), both of whom received the message and responded rather quickly. Yesterday I spoke on video chat with dear beloved friends in New Delhi. Earlier today I was watching the CCTV News (China Central Television) online. Last week I listened to an EDM podcast from Egypt, and swapped a Tarot reading for a Canadian friend's psychic reading. Isn't it amazing that we can do all this?!

While occurrences like these can easily be taken for granted, particularly by members of younger generations (like me!), it's honestly miraculous that global communication can be transmitted instantaneously. Humanity has never seen this before. While there's no telling what the future holds, the present moment is unlike anything we've ever seen. Younger generations in the western world tend to be incredibly proficient at screen-based communication, yet are often encounter obstacles when faced with person-to-person dialogue. Our level of immediate communication has reached such a fever pitch that it's almost *unique* for you to be reading these words in a real-life paper magazine.

One of the most well known occult definitions of magick is by English occultist Aleister Crowley, who said, "Magick is the science and art of causing change to occur in conformity with Will." Crowley, whose work actually aided the creation of Wicca more than is generally known, used "Will" in the sense of one's individual destiny or higher truth. Thelema, a movement founded by Crowley, uses the axiom *Do what thou Wilt shall be the whole of the Law*. This is also the most likely source for the portion of the Wiccan Rede that reads *Do as ye will*. This, then, does not mean "do whatever you want," but instead means that our everyday lives and our magickal workings should express our higher spiritual callings; our Will; our Destiny; our Dharma.

Mail, of one kind or another, has been in existence for as long as we innovative humans have utilised written communication. Utilising the physical plane for our magick (old-fashioned snail-mail!), we can help create potentially reverberating positive change simply by writing a letter. According to the Crowleyan or Thelemic definition of magick (which is also where we get the "k" now commonly used in the word *magick*), simply writing a letter or postcard to a company would be a great way to harness change by physical means. Emails are empty in many ways. When we get postal mail we can feel the energy or personality of the person sending the letter or item – unless, of course, it's mass-manufactured junk mail – but never mind that! Postal mail is a magickal thing, and has the potential to carry great amounts of energy and power from point A to point B. It's also the only form of long-distance communication that is *confidential*, as phones and emails can be tapped. For less than 50 cents (at the time of this writing, in America), we can write a few-paged letter (or what-have-you), stick it in a mailbox, and kick back with some red wine while it zips across the country in a few days. That truly is amazing. Especially with wine.

So, how can someone work their magick through snail-mail? Let's start by looking at something that most people don't think of as necessarily "magickal."

Postcards are the most likely form of mail to get read by ultra-large corporations and high-rolling political entities. Postcards can be quickly written and are very inexpensive to send. If someone is receiving mounds upon mounds of mail, they are more likely to read the postcards before opening letters. However, both can be effective and both have their times and places.

Corporations and political institutions often regard *one* individual's opinion as the voice of *many* more. One consumer's feedback is seen as reflecting the views of hundreds or thousands of additional consumers, depending on the market or population. Most people never take the time to make corporate contact. By taking a few minutes to express sentiments, a company or institution may be more liable to change in progressive ways. It literally only takes a few minutes and a bit of couch-change to pay for a stamp. In my opinion, this is an incredibly small sacrifice for a piece of activism that could potentially have rippling effects that could help people, animals, or the earth. Is this not our duty as magicians and seekers of expanded awareness?

My Coven and I enjoy sending "care packages" to friends and relatives around the world, whether at Yuletide, harvest time, when someone falls ill, or whenever the mood takes us. Sharing is caring. Care packages can be a fun and creative act of personal magick; simply piece together a number of fun items from around the house or from local shops, write a note, channel energies of your choice into the package, seal it up, and send off the love. It's a fun experience to open a random package of random stuff, especially if it's imbued with intentions of bonding, support, or healing.

It can also be fun to create a spiritual piece of art that is built in collaboration with a friend at a distance. Begin the piece - regardless of the medium - and mail it to your friend to add to, alter, and imbue. They can mail it back to you to do the same.

This can continue for as long as you wish, until you both feel the piece is a completed work of magickal art that carries the intentions you set forth to create.

Postal magick is something I've utilized in some of the Men's Rituals I've hosted for the the "Dark Sun." In the multicultural temple I cofounded, called Opus Aima Obscuræ (OAO), we utilise the Dark Sun or New Sun as the masculine equivalent to the women's Dark Moon or New Moon. This occurs when the sun enters a new zodiac sign in common tropical astrology.

During a ritual marking the sun's entrance into Virgo (a sign ruled by Mercury, a planet/god of communication), we once performed postcard magick for the Men's Ritual. Each of us took a small stack of postcards and visualised a place we wished to travel at some point in the future. Upon creating this traveling bucket list, we performed a series of magickal exercises to enchant and empower the postcards, which were to be mailed to those destinations. Magick included the creation of sigils to represent these traveling goals. (Please note that there are multiple ways to create a sigil or magickal seal aligned to a specific purpose. Please consult a book or Internet source for more information on sigilry, particularly the methods given by Austin Osman Spare. Also, my friend Laura Tempest Zakroff wrote a wonderful new book called *Sigil Witchery*!) Our sigils that us men created in the ritual represented these personal goals, acting a visual anchors for our intentions, which were worded in the form of "I will effortlessly and joyously travel to _____ in this lifetime," or similar affirmations.

Once the sigils were created, drawn, and enchanted on the left sides of the postcards, the symbols were layered overtop in a series of fun stickers like smiley faces and hearts. Many of these stickers entirely covered up any given sigil. On the right side of each postcard, the address was written. We researched addresses of hotels in any given national or global location we picked for these "travel spells," and addressed them as such. For example, if I wanted to travel to Ireland I would research a functioning hotel in Ireland and address it to the hotel – this would ensure the postcard's delivery to the city or country of manifestation. Additionally, we wrote a bit of text on the left sides of each postcard so that the postcards wouldn't look *too* suspicious or strange - the goal is not to scare the randomised recipient! Because these were being sent to hotels, each postcard got a silly little message, like, "Thanks for the great stay! Love your hotel! Cheers!" or we simply made it look as if a child had written the postcard and an adult addressed it.

To conclude, each participant used a sterile diabetic lancet to prick the pointer finger of his left hand (to represent the future, and the fiery command of one's own energy) and put a small "blood stamp" in the right-hand uppermost part of the postcard. Once dried, proper national or international postage was secured atop the blood prints, leaving the blood magick hidden underneath the postage stamps.

Raven Digitalis Author of Esoteric Empathy

To summarise, each of these were magically charged, odd-but-happy looking postcards addressed to hotels across the globe. The postcards we had chosen had pleasant nature scenes on the front sides of each. The postcards were properly stamped depending on the area they were being mailed to (postage rates can be looked up online), and no postcards had a return address (this *anonymity* is important with this sort of magick). Postcards should be put in a public mailbox, not mailed from your place of residence, as to send off these energies without an obvious link to your person.

When each hotel receives any given postcard, it's likely that the recipient would briefly read the postcard, look at it strangely, perhaps give a little chuckle, and then toss it in the trash. Once tossed in the trash, it ensures that the magician's energy, through the sigil and blood-print, is connected to the location being manifested for travel. If the address of the hotel is expired, the post office in that area will simply "dead letter" the postcard, which will also make its way into the trash. The magician, then, can choose when to astrally connect to the city or country of choice, helping pull the area closer energetically, thus making travelling to that location easier with time.

However you choose to utilise the postal system to carry your magick, give thanks to Mercury, Hermes, or Thoth: three of the classical gods of communication. It would be quite appropriate to draw the alchemical symbol for Mercury on pieces of mail that is, itself, a spell. This not only ensures safe delivery, but aligns the essence of the god to the postal system itself, giving thanks for the miracles of modern communication.

Raven Digitalis (Missoula, MT, USA) is the author of *The Everyday Empath, Esoteric Empathy, Shadow Magick Compendium, Planetary Spells & Rituals* and *Goth Craft* (Llewellyn Worldwide). He is the co-founder of a nonprofit multicultural temple called Opus Aima Obscuræ (OAO), which primarily observes NeoPagan and Hindu traditions. Raven has been an earth-based practitioner since 1999, a Priest since 2003, a Freemason since 2012, and an empath all of his life. He holds a degree in cultural anthropology from the University of Montana and is also a professional Tarot reader, DJ, card-carrying magician, small-scale farmer and animal rights advocate.
www.ravendigitalis.com   www.facebook.com/ravendigitalis   www.opusaimaobscurae.org   www.facebook.com/opusaimaobscurae

Divine Feminine

BAAL KADMON

Since the dawn of time, our ancient ancestors knew intuitively that the Divine Feminine is the source of all life. Although there are depictions of the Divine Masculine in ancient inscriptions and carvings, it is the Divine Feminine that stands out. Some notable examples are the Venus figurines that have been found throughout Europe and much of Eurasia. A recent find in the Golan Heights in Israel has been dated back to as late as 230,000 B.C.; some other figures may be much older.

As the Mother Goddess, she embodies all, for she gives birth to all. It is through the Divine Feminine that all have come into being. She is tireless in her life-vivifying and life-giving capacities. Whole worlds come in and out of existence because of, and due to her bountiful essence.

When I first embarked on my spiritual journey as a teenager, I was not as drawn initially to the demons and Gods. I was drawn and enamoured by the Goddess. One of my first forays into Magick and Mystery was with the Goddess Isis. She was and still is, my patron. She opened my eyes to so many things. I owe much of who I am today to her. In time, the Feminine Divine worked on me in her various forms. She called me to work with her as the Goddess Tara, in all her forms. Tara nurtured me through many difficult moments in my life and nudged me when I needed it most.

As I grew in experience and in years, life became more complex. I made many mistakes in my life, and it was then she appeared again to me, but as Lilith, as Tiamat, and as Kali. Her powerful and wrathful aspect nudged me and pushed me to make the changes that I needed to make in my life. Despite the harshness of her gaze, her embrace has always remained warm to me. Never has her extended hand grown cold to the touch.

As I further matured, she came to me as the Mother Mary, and it was here that much of our work together took place. Much of this work is and shall remain close to my heart.

When I reflect on my years as a practitioner of the Occult and Magick, I realised more and more why the divine feminine was so alluring to me. She represents the harmonising forces of existence like no other can. She is not only the life-bringer, but she is also desolation and death. We in the West are fearful of ferocity in the feminine. This is because there is a misunderstanding of what ferocity is. In Western Canon, ferocity is evil, while being demure and passive are viewed as the ultimate virtues. However, when you look at nature, what do you see? What do you experience? You see and experience beautiful flowers and refreshing breezes but turn your head even slightly, and you will also see and experience man-eating tigers, venomous snakes, and microbial life that lie in wait. Neither of these experiences of nature can be called "Good" nor "Evil," they just are; both convey the vulnerability of the Divine Feminine in their own way.

It is no coincidence that in the East, she is the embodiment of Kundalini, she is Shakti, the life essence of not only our body and mind, but of the entire universe. It is in Kundalini that we further see her all-encompassing power. From some, she uncoils slowly and ascends through the Chakras; each Chakra is opening up like a Lotus petal, one by one. For others, she bursts forth through them, creating havoc, Chaos and destruction.

This, to me, is the Goddess, and it is for this reason nearly all my private work is with her in many of her aspects, both left and right.

I feel that to embrace the Goddess truly, vulnerability is vital. When she calls on you, and you heed her call, she will hold your hand and guide you through the path you are on. Just like water over time will carve rock, slowly, she makes her way through you. Or, if you are in a time in your life that sight is dim, and ego is bright, she can crash through you like a Rogue Wave that jumps out at you without warning, breaking you open. I have experienced both of these things.

Considering this, I would like to say that the Goddess isn't about balance. The Goddess is about harmony in all things. Most confuse balance and harmony, but they are very different. If you look upon a balanced scale, what do you see? You see nothing. You see something that is lifeless and static. The Goddess is harmony, the ebb and flow of things. When there is winter, there will be summer, and when there is life, there is also death. This is a harmonising process, not a balanced, static one. If it were static, they would be even, but as we know, life is never even. A Fractal, the underlying pattern of life is not even, and it is not a straight line nor is it smooth. As Benoit Mandelbrot said, "Smooth shapes are very rare in the wild, but extremely important in the ivory tower…"

I feel the key to truly working with the Goddess is to suspend judgment of what and how she appears to you as a practitioner. For example, she has appeared to me as the Mother Mary, yet for some, if she appeared this way, they would doubt her. They would turn their backs on her because there is such hostility against manifestations that may be counter to an entrenched and idolatrous notion in the mind. It is when she comes to you in a way that teases the discomfort out of you, that is when your work with her is needed most. We must get out of the Ivory tower of the mind in order to hear her call.

This turning away from what makes us uncomfortable reminds me of what the great Christian Mystic Meister Eckhart said, "God is at home, it is we who have gone out for a walk."

I couldn't agree more. The Goddess is at home; it is we who have gone out for a walk. It is time to come home.

So Mote it Be!

Bio:

Baal Kadmon is an Author, Occultist, and teacher based out of New York City. In addition to the Occult, he is a scholar of Religion, Philosophy, and a Historian specializing in Ancient History, Late Antiquity and Medieval History. He has studies Israeli Hebrew, Classical Hebrew, Ugaritic language, Arabic, Judeo-Aramaic, Syriac, Ancient Greek and Classical Latin.

Baal first discovered his occult calling when he was very young. It was only in his teens, when on a trip to the Middle East that he heeded the call. Several teachers and many decades later he felt ready to share what he had learned.

His teachings are unconventional. In addition to rituals, he includes in-depth history in almost all the books that he writes. He shatters the beloved and idolatrously held notions most occultists hold dear. His pared-down approach to Magick is refreshing and is very much needed in a field that is mired by self-important magicians and teachers who place more importance on pomp and circumstance, than on Magick and self-inquiry.

You can reach him at the following sites:

Main site: www.baalkadmon.com

For Video Courses, please go to: https://www.occultcourses.com

For Brainwave Audios, please go to: https://www.occultmindscapes.com

For Meditation Audios, Please go to: https://www.quantumsynchrony.com

A Site dedicated to Saint Expedite. please go to: https://www.saintexpedite.com

NEPTUNE'S SCEPTRE
Part 4 of our Erotic Pagan Fiction by DD Scarlet

Welcome to Salacia, Island of Sensuality.
Our Heroines have arrived at "Neptune's Haven," a bungalow style beach resort on an unspoiled island paradise. Here you can enjoy pristine beaches, hike through the mysterious jungle, paddle in tropical ponds by day or romantic moonlight swims at night. On Salacia, you will be treated to a sensual spa styled pampering each and every day and so much more…

https://ddscarlet.weebly.com

Rainaa didn't close her eyes, instead her alertness still with her, she just continued to stare at him. Then she noticed not just the sparkling of his incredible eyes, but jewels beginning to appear on his forehead. She slowly reached up to validate their actuality. "There… there's jewels," she observed as she pulled back from his kiss.

"They're not jewels – they're scales," Koa corrected.

"They're pretty," she said as she touched them with her fingertips. Koa sighed before leaning in to kiss her again. Rainaa then allowed her eyes to close also, briefly succumbing to his kiss. Her body was so on fire – her breasts lusciously sensitive, her pussy – slippery, hot and throbbing… His mouth was warm and moist and she enjoyed the feel of it encompassing her own. Gently she stroked his forehead, touching the scales, until she was sure that more had grown… She opened her eyes. There was now a spray of them across his forehead and temples and on the square of his jaw. She noticed them forming sparsely on his shoulders and she traced their smoothness over to the centre of his back. Her breaths were deep and steady, apprehensive of what was happening before her very eyes.

Koa saw the fear in her eyes and quickly engaged her in another adoring kiss, as he pulled her securely against him and began to walk them back into slightly deeper water. Somewhere between his kiss and his thickening scent she began to experience euphoria, and then the butterflies and twinging in her abdomen increased. "Relax," he spoke huskily through their kiss, "Just allow it to happen, Rainaa…"

As he kissed her she could feel the flutters in her stomach and they in turn seemed to cause an intense pulsating in her pussy and she suddenly moaned and Koa moaned also in response. Slowly he continued to walk them deeper into the water, until they were standing – Rainaa, waist deep. She pressed her needing body against him, her breasts and hard nipples sensitive to the texture of his flesh, and then she began to trace her hand over the scales forming down the centreline of his back when suddenly she discovered something protruding from between his shoulder blades. She instantly pulled back.

"What are you?" she asked, but Koa just looked at her fondly. "Are you a merman?" She then bravely stroked what seemed to be a billowing fin on his back, when suddenly it flicked and stiffened, taking form.

"No… Not anymore… I am The Sceptre," he told her, his tone peaceful.

"The what?"

"I am… We, the other hosts and I, collectively, are Neptune's Sceptre. We sacrificed our existence as Merpeople for a holier purpose."

"What purpose?"

"To ensure the balance between Neptune and the Earth… To help humans to give back to the King of fertility… So the karma between you remains balanced, and abundance may be yours always."

"The Ritual of Salacia? The spawning..?"

"Yes."

"Am I to be sacrificed?" Rainaa asked, alarmed.

"No, Neptune is about giving life – not taking it away…" Koa smiled at her affectionately, reassuring her of her safety.

"Your scales are melting…"

"No, they are billowing… Releasing sex pheromones and making them pleasant for you to touch."

She stared at him in awe and then continued to touch his back, as if searching for proof. Then she allowed her hand to follow the scales all the way down to the small of his back - her touch stirring his libido, and he kissed her. She found where the fabric was sitting on his hips and she felt the texture beneath it. Koa reached down with one hand and unhooked the loosely tied fabric, allowing it to float away on the waves. Out of curiosity she had to ask, "Do you have a tail?"

"Yes" Koa replied.

Rainaa looked down to where the water was lapping at his waist, and nervously she asked, "C-can I s-s-see it?"

Koa smiled breathtakingly and said, "Sure," and then he collected her in his arms and circled his tail around beside her, Rainaa noticing the swirl of water. Then he flipped it up and cradled it around behind her shoulders before splashing it back into the water.

Rainaa wasn't sure what she really expected to see but the initial sight of Koa's tail shocked her! She gasped and began to shake, her eyes wide like saucers. "Holy fuck!" she exclaimed.

"You are perfectly safe, Rainaa," Koa scooped her against his chest and thrust his tail, pushing them out to slightly deeper water. "I would never hurt you."

She brushed her hand over his hip and felt the billowing scales, fluttering in the water, soft under her fingertips. "This is really happening, isn't it?" she said, "I mean all of it…"

"Yes Rainaa… We are going to start spawning soon," and then he collected her face to his and sighed in deep lust as he kissed her. She kissed him back, her breasts and lower abdomen quivering. He lowered his mouth to one of her breasts and took the hard nipple into the warmth and just suckled on it and Rainaa moaned out loud – the twinging in her abdomen intensifying. Then he let that one go and took her other nipple into his mouth…

"Koa..?" she said on breathy whispers.

"Yes?"

"How are you going to have sex with me?" she asked and he looked up at her peacefully. "Your bottom half is a fish."

"The Sceptre are a little different from the Mer – Neptune adapted us to be able to carry out our task. But even the Mer are warm blooded and have penises," Koa cupped her face and kissed her, "But my penis was designed especially to penetrate and stimulate a human female's cervix, relaxing it so that the eggs may pass through…"

"What?" Rainaa asked, gobsmacked and trembling again with concern.

"Rainaa…"

"Will it damage me..? My insides?"

"No!"

"Koa, I'm afraid," she expressed.

"You don't need to be…" he assured her before taking her hand and gently guiding it down over the ripples of his six pack to where she indeed found a cock. Koa saw her milky skin flush in the moonlight, but still she smiled.

Rainaa tickled the base of his cock in admiration and then her breaths deepened as she dared to trail her fingers along his impressive length, before delicately sliding them around the girth and gently massaging it.

Koa removed the fabric from her and allowed it to drift away before lifting her bottom, pulling her hips to him and curling her legs around him. Curious, she slowly ran her feet down and back up his tail, his captivating, billowing scales tickling her soles. Then, her lower abdomen aching, she boldly glided her finger along to the tip of the cock and felt the slim three inch extension, and she knew that Koa wasn't lying and that he really was designed to penetrate her cervix and help her spawn.

Rainaa raised one arm to his burly shoulder and the other to his head and she began kissing him. She naturally pressed her own billowing petals against his shaft and just experienced its external presence, its warmth and smooth texture making her lust unapologetically.

Koa kissed her deeply, his scales releasing more pheromones as he did so and Rainaa's abdomen began to twinge mercilessly making her moan in pain. She could feel her body craving the connection he described. She could feel the eggs lodging against the inner side of her cervix, unyielding and demanding to be released, and then she started to cry out, push her pelvis forward and tilt her head back. "Are you ready for me now, Rainaa?"

Raina found it hard to talk, instead she just groaned and pushed herself against him and planted her mouth hungrily over his. Then to her absolute relief she felt him tilt her hips and push his member inside of her. She felt every muscle in her stomach tense and shudder, as her body hungrily welcomed him, but still that infernal twinging continued.

She grasped his shoulders and moved herself on his phallus, itching for him to go deeper, and then she sensed it and she froze and her legs just quivered as she felt the tip of his penis, via way of little rapid strokes, gradually work its way through her cervix and she started crying out in some kind of ecstasy, feeling utterly impaled, and she just hung loosely around his neck, somehow happily captive.

Koa also began to pant and groan and then kissed the side of her neck before informing her, "Rainaa, I need to take you to the spawning pool now..." He looked at her and witnessed her expression of both shock and anguished need and he quickly, passionately kissed her. "Remember I said we are polygynandrous?" She listened but she didn't speak, "But tonight Rainaa... You will feel no fear, and no shame... Tonight you will just spawn for Neptune, okay? Now hold on."

Find our more about the mysterious merpeople of the Island of Salacia as DD Scarlet continues her Pagan tale with us next issue!

IMAGE CREDIT Imre Zsido. See more on page 36

Magick Magazine No. 10

THE SOUTHERN & NORTHERN WITCH'S ALMANAC

FEBRUARY - DECEMBER 2020

Sacred Days - Ancient Festivals - Commemorative Dates
Moon Phases - Astronomical Alignments

All Collated In One Place For Your Easy Reference

by Shé D'Montford

Know when and why to work your magick by following Magick Magazine's almanac

All times are Australian Eastern Standard Time (AEST - UTC +10) - add 1 hour for Daylight Savings Time when applicable.

FEBRUARY

1 ✪ **Major Sabbat LAMMAS** in the Southern Hemisphere - Northern Hemisphere **Imbolc**, the 3-day Celtic festival marking the period of lactation of the ewes.

Lammas is the festival of light. The God Lugh's Day (Lughnasadh) when he returns light to the world. Plough Sunday, Rogation days, **Lammas** Day (Anglo-Saxon hlaf-mas, "loaf-mass"), also known as Loaf Mass Day, is a Christian holiday celebrated in some English-speaking countries in the Northern Hemisphere on 1 August.

Festival Of Brigit, Brigantia/Brighid the Celtic Goddess of healing, fertility, and patroness of smiths. She ushers Spring to the land after The Cailleach's winter reign. Children make hanging mobiles with the day old crosses and use other food items to represent the sun, the moon, and the stars. It is believed that a wisp of straw or rushes left over from the making of the crosses the night before, under the mattress or pillow wards off disease. Strands from it were tied about an aching head, a sore limb during and fishermen carried it when at sea. **The Wives' Feast Day** honours Brighid in the Highlands of Scotland and north England the festival is strictly matriarchal - the door of the feasting place was barred to the men of the community who had to plead humbly to honour Bride.

The Queen Comes to the Mound. A procession to the sacred spring, the Swallowhead of **Sul/Minerva** when the spring starts flowing again in February. She heals with an ashless fire in her sanctuary. This also happens for the Goddess of Silbury Hill.

The Lesser Eleusinian Mysteries – Eleusinian Mysteries celebrated the return of Persephone/Kore to her mother Demeter after her descent into underworld where she was the wife of Pluto, its King.

02. 11:42 ☽ First Quarter

Juno Februa - The Purifier - Roman custom of burning candles to the goddess Februa, mother of Mars, to scare away evil spirits.

The Day of the Virgin Mary was attached to Lupercalia or Candlemas, because many candles were lit on that day as had been done for centauries at the festival of Proserpine, whom her mother Ceres sought with candles.

Groundhog Day- America.
Waitangi Day. New Zealand

09. 17:33 ○ Full Moon

11. 06:30 ○ Moon Perigee: 360500 km

11. Our Lady of Lourdes [French] Bernadette Soubirous had visions of Mary in the Grotto at Lourdes. It had in previous centuries been a shrine to the Goddess–cult. The herb, which grew in the cave that Bernadette ate in the course of her guided actions, was a sacred in the bygone cult. The young girl who witnessed the visions drew forth a stream of healing water from the mud. The Lesser Mystery of Lourdes, mimicked The Lesser Eleusinian Mysteries.

12. The Festival of Artemis- the Greek Goddess of the hunt (known as Diana to the Romans).

Gerald Gardiner – anniversary of the death of the founder of the Gardinerian tradition, who many consider one of the fathers of the modern Wicca, on this day in 1964.

13. The Parentalis and the **Feralia-** the 7day festival of the **Manes**, the Roman spirits of the dead, who inhabit the underworld.

15. The Lupercalia- the festival of Lupa, The She-Wolf which suckled Romulus and Remus, and Faunus, the Roman god of flocks, fertility and wild nature Priests (called the Luperci) wearing skins walked through the streets of Rome and hit the spectators with belts made from goat skin

St Valentine is the name of a singing Christian priest that fell in love with a pagan emperors daughter and was condemned to death for wanting to be 'Her Valentine.' His random and reckless love was commemorated with a lottery of willing young ladies, whose names were put in a box and drawn to randomly be the dates for the years up coming festivities. These were also called Valentines. It was considered to be an omen of later being man and wife. This turned into the giving of cards and chocolates in the Victorian era.

16. 08:17 ☾ Last Quarter.

The Festival Of Fornax, the Roman Goddess of bread making.

The Quirinalia, the festival of Quirinus, an earlier Roman god of war.

17 ☿ Mercury Retrograde in Pisces

Celtic Tree Moon of ASH

February 18 - March 17

18. 23:18 ○ Moon- ♂ Mars: 0.8° S.

Spenta Armaiti Festival of women and of cultivation celebrated by the Zoroastrians.

20. 05:36 ○ Moon- ♃ Jupiter: 1° N,

23:47 ○ Moon- ♄ Saturn: 1.9° N.

22. The Festival Of The Goddess Concordia, the patron of good will and favour.

23. The Terminalia, the festival of Terminus, the Roman god of boundaries and border markers.

24. 01:32 ● New Moon

26. 21:35 ○ Moon Apogee: 406300 km.

Day of Mut [Egyptian] the powerfully protecting, primordial Vulture Goddess of Upper Egypt. Some times in her lioness form the wife of the God Amun of Karnak. The High–Priestess Queen of Egypt wore the Vulture Goddess Mut as a head–dress to signify her spiritual development, the expansion of her brain, the opening of the third eye, and the blending of her head with the Goddess of Life and Death Herself.

27. 21:51 ○ Moon- ♀ Venus: 7° N.

MARCH

01. **The Kalends-** New Year's Day in the old Roman calendar. Sacred to Vesta/Isis a new fire is lighted in her secret shrine, and the rekindled only by a bale fire burning or by the primitive friction method of boring a piece of wood from a fruit tree.

Juno Lucina, The Matronalia- A pagan mothers day - Primary feast of Juno, the chief Roman goddess. A festival celebrated by Roman matrons on the 1st of March, the anniversary of the foundation of the temple of Juno Lucina on the Esquiline. In the houses, prayers were offered for a prosperous wedlock, the women received presents from the men and waited on the slaves, just as the men did at the Saturnalia. In the temple of the Goddess, women and girls prayed to her and brought pious offerings. At this festival, Juno was represented veiled, with a flower in her right hand and an infant in swaddling clothes in her left.

Feriae Marti - The festival of the Gods of war. Literally, "The Festival of Mars," was a 25-day festival to the Roman god of war and the protector of the farmer's land and his crops. We derive the term Martial arts from Mars' own priest called the Flamen Martialis. His other priest the *Salii*, the "Leaping Priests" or the "Dancing Priests," would perform Cossack or Break-Dancing style martial arts displays in the streets until the 24th of the Month. The last nine days of this period were also fast days. On the 25th of the Month, the Romans broke their fast at the *Hilaria* "Festival of Joy."

02. **Holy Wells Day-** the day of Ceadda, the Celtic goddess of healing springs and holy wells.

Magha Puja Day -Major Buddhist festival.

05:57 ☽ First Quarter.

04. First official neo-pagan church established 1968 by Oberon Zell -The Church of all Worlds Anniversary.

05. **Festival of The Ship of Isis-** is held in recognition of her being the patroness of navigation and inventress of the sail. The term "carnival" comes from the Latin name for this

festival - Currus Navalis. It was a grand procession of carts or cars that had 'floats' on them to the sea where the priest offered the Goddess a beautifully built ship, with Egyptian hieroglyphics over the entire hull after he purified it with a torch, an egg and sulphur. The sail was white linen that bore a prayer to the Queen of the Stars, the Mother of the Season, and the Mistress of the Universe for her protection of shipping during the new sailing season.

The Pond of the Goddess is still celebrated in the Islamic world, in Africa, and is called "The Pond of Fatima, the daughter of the Prophet." In the procession, one man is dressed as Anubis with a face black on one side and gold on the other, five carry a wine jar. Behind them dances a man carrying on his shoulders, the statue representing the Goddess as the beautiful Mother of us all. Then comes a priest with a box containing the secret implements of her wonderful cult. Another priest carries a very interesting emblem of her Godhead: a vessel of burnished gold covered in Egyptian hieroglyphics. It has rounded bottom, a long spout, and a curving handle along which is an asp raising its head displaying its wrinkled, puffed-out throat.

10. 03:48 ○ Full Moon,

16:33 ○ Moon Perigee: 357100 km

12. **Hypatia Memorial Day- The 1st Pagan Martyr-** On this day in 415 AD Hypatia of Alexandria was scraped and sliced to bits with cockleshells by the mad monks of the Nitre Desert of Libya, despite her intimacy with Orestes, the city's Prefect. It is thought that the high nitrate content of their desert surroundings could have contributed to their hysteria but there were also political motivations. Many saw Hypatia as a priestess/ representative of Aphrodite because she became the recognised head of the Neo-Platonist School at Alexandria. She attracted many pupils due to her eloquence, rare modesty, great beauty and her remarkable intellectual gifts including leading her field in philosophy, astronomy, mathematics and geometry. She was held as an oracle for her wisdom, being consulted by magistrates in important cases. After her murder many Pagan scholars fled from Alexandria. This marked the beginning of the dark ages.

13. **Witch's Annual Lucky Day, Dakini Day-** a celebration of magickal women in Tibet. A Dakini is a female who opens to those that knock (seeking knowledge) - the highest form of magickal teacher. **Birth date of Diotima-** a celebration of a tradition of women as teachers of the greatest Pagan philosophers upon which Western civilisation is based. Diotima was the teacher of Socrates, described by him as "a woman wise in this ravel and in many other kinds of knowledge." (Plato, Symposium, p201d.) There are many other important women teachers who are celebrated on this day… too many to list in full. This is a day to honour pagan women who made a magical

difference to your community or to society in large.

14. **Equirria-** a festival in honour of Mars, the god of war. Horse races were held on this day.

15. **The Festival of Anna Perenna-** the Roman goddess of the circle of the year. Her festival was celebrated on the full moon of the first month of the Roman year i.e. The Ides of March. **Kybele/Rhea-** [Anatolian] 1week-long purification for the Rites of Kybele that ends on 22nd March, marked by a procession of reed-bearers to her lioness throne.

16. 19:34 ☾ Last Quarter.

Celtic day of Morgan LeFay- which became the Christian **St. Patrick's Day**. His removing the snakes from Ireland is a metaphor for the key role he played in removing the indigenous magickal priestess tradition epitomised by this day being remembered by his name not the High Priestess' title. **Tristeria** (Related to the word hysteria) was an ancient Greek festival to honour Dionysus, God of wine and relief from pain. Held in secret and originally attended by women only, for two-three days. These festivals celebrated the emergence of Dionysus from the underworld, with wild orgies in the mountains. The first day of which was presided over by the Maenads, in their state of Mainomenos, (from which we derive our terms 'mania' and 'madness'). The second day saw the Bacchic Nymphs in their Thyiadic, or raving, state, a more sensual, and benign Bacchanal assisted by satyrs, though still orgiastic. Some explain these rites were a release of psychological repression, as the ancients claim that the Maenads, or wild women, were the resisters of the Bacchic urge, sent mad, while the Thyiades, or ravers, had accepted the Dionysian ecstasy and kept their sanity. This also included the festivities of the grape harvest, and its carnivalesque ritual processions from the vineyards to the wine press. It was at these times that initiations into the Mysteries were held.

17. **The Liberalia**, the festival of Liber and Libera, a Roman fertility god and Goddess.

18.

Celtic Tree Moon of ALDER

Gaelic - Fearn - March 18 - April 14
Alder brides the magickal space between both heaven and earth. A time for making spiritual decisions, magick relating to prophecy and divination. Alder flowers and twigs are known as charms to be used in Faerie magick. Whistles were once made out of Alder shoots to call upon Air spirits, so it's an ideal wood for making a pipe or flute.

18. 18:19 ○ Moon- 4Mars: 0.8° N.

Celtic day of Argante, Sheela-Ne-Nag Day- This ancient Irish fertility and overt sexuality Goddess was traditionally honoured on this day until she was adopted by the Christians as the Mother (or sometimes the consort) of Saint Patrick.

19. 10:04 ○ Moon- ♄ Saturn: 2.3° N. **Hindu New Year - Ramayana** begins - This Hindu celebration goes for 9 days. **Lesser Panathen Quinquatria** − Day one of five days. Birthday of Athena but also of wisdom, arts and trades and **Quinquatrus** the older Roman god of war. In later times it moved to the spring, because of Roman influence, in order to make it correspond to the Quinquatrus of Minerva.

20. 13:50 **Vernal Equinox,**

✡ Major Sabbat MABON

Autumal Equinox in the southern hemisphere. **Ostara** - Spring Equinox in the northern hemisphere and was the ancient Middle Eastern New Year's Day. Celtic celebration of the bare fields after the harvest. The laying alcohol down to mature is the celebration of John Barleycorn "We have reaped what we have sown."

20:22 ♂ Mars- ♃ Jupiter: 0.7° N.

Pelusia- An Egyptian Festival fundamental in the cult of Isis, securing the next annual inundation of the Nile by sympathetic magick.

21. **Norouz** (New Year) - Persian/ Zoroastrian.

22. 03:48 ○ Moon-1Mercury: 4° N. **Inanna/Ishtar/Belat-**Their festivals are on the second day of the middle-eastern month of Nisan. **Isis/Bastet** The priests wore black cassock in the service of Isis at this festival. They used the cross as a symbol of her husband's and son's suffering and rang bells, timbrel or sistrum to stir the resurrection of them both. **Gardens of Adonis** celebrates Aphrodite/Venus and Adonis and the dying or dead lover of Astarte. This festival was celebrated with baskets or pots filled with earth, in which wheat, barley, lettuces, fennel and various kinds of flowers were grown and tended for eight days, chiefly or exclusively by women after which they make offerings to the strong Goddess. At Easter, Sicilian women sow wheat and lentils in plates, which they keep in the dark and water every two days. The plants soon shoot up, then 12 of the stalks are tied together with red ribbons, and the plates containing them are placed on graves on Good Friday, just as the gardens of Adonis were placed on the grave of the dead Adonis. The whole custom is a continuation of the worship of Adonis.

23. **A Festival Of Mars And Nerine-** the marriage of Mars to the Sabine goddess whom people identified with Athena/Minerva or Aphrodite/Venus. **Tubilustrium-**Another festival in honour of Mars. On this, day weapons and war-trumpets were cleansed.

24.11:59 ☿ Mercury Elongation:27.8° W. **The Rites of Venus Urania/ Astarte and Adonis at Byblos-** all the people in mourning enter a deep cavern, where the image of a young man lies on a bed of flowers and herbs. Whole days are passed in prayer and lamentation. **Adonia-** were solemn feasts in honour of Venus, and in memory of her beloved Adonis.

They lasted two days. **Ishtar and Tammuz-** the Goddess descended to the underworld to bring back her youthful husband from the dead. Women mourned for the dead god in Babylon.

25. 01:23 ○ Moon Apogee: 406700 km, 07:59 ♀ Venus Elongation:46.1°E.

The Hilaria: the festival of Joy-the divine resurrections were celebrated with a wild outburst of glee. The God of joy, Hilaritus was invoked. This became **Passion Sunday** for the Christians. The day before had seen rites of the wildest sorrow; they sought and mourned for Attis on the mountains. On the 3rd day, he was found again, the image of the Goddess Kybele was purified from the contagion of death, and a feast of joy was celebrated as wild as had been the days of sorrow.

Eostre/Easter derives the word from Eostre, Northumberland spelling of Eastre stara, the Saxon goddess of spring, another form of Astarté the Sumerian fertility goddess whose festival was celebrated in Europe at the vernal equinox by cheering "Wassail. Hail and be whole, be well!" as a salutation over the spiced-ale cup, that was drunk on the day when the civil and legal year ended and began again on March 25th. It was not until as late as1752, the historic year was changed to January 1st. In Scotland, the legal year was changed to January 1st in 1600.

26. **Mabon's Day-** Celtic.

The Requietio of Kybele- is mentioned in the Calendar of Philocalus, written in the year 354, as the day following the Hlaria as a day of rest.

Demeter and Persephone brings back the life of spring in the form of a tree or a maiden, summoned to rise from the sleeping Earth.

The Irish Grey Woman of Crotlieve, a pillar stone set up in prehistoric times is elaborately dressed up like a woman for the Easter festivities.

Khordad Sal Birth of Prophet Zaranhushtra – Zoroastrian.

28. **Ramanavami-**the end of the 9 day Ramayana festival – Hindu.

Spells performed to Ishtar for the healing of sick man: *"In the month of Tammuz, when Ishtar causes the people of the land to weep for Tammuz, her husband, then, when the families of humankind are gathered together there, Ishtar appears, and, beholding the situation of humankind, takes away sickness and causes sickness. On the twenty-eighth day of the month, the day of sheep-folds, thou shalt offer a vulva of lapis-lazuli and a golden star to Ishtar; thou shalt name the name of the sick man and say, "Deliver the sick man"*

29. **The Hieros Gamos-** or Holy Marriage was the most significant rite of the New Year. The symbolic wedding between the king, who represented the god Dumuzi, and a priestesses, who represented the Goddess Inanna, was to be the dominant partner, since She makes him king. **Basilissa** -the most

important Greek ceremony of the Anthesteria. A moveable feast where a local king pays Ishtar to bestow upon him his regal authority. The marriage of the Basileus or wife of the Archon Basileus, with Dionysus, the Basilissa regarded as representing the country. The ceremony took place in the older of the two temples of the Lenaeon, which was never opened except on this occasion. **Ishtar's Day**-sacred to the ancient Babylonian Goddess of Love.
Festival of Salus- the Goddess of salt, salaries, greetings, safety and wellbeing. Optimum time for personal protection spells.
31. **Aradian festival of Luna-** originally a Thracian Goddess of the moon and Magick. The Greeks identified her as Artemis, Hecate and Persephone. The worship of this imported Goddess was so popular that it became a state ceremonial at Athens, a public torch lit festival called the Bendideia. Eventually she became the Italian Goddess of the Moon and has an ancient sanctuary in Rome today.
Mawlid an Nabi-Islam -The birthday of Prophet Muhammad, founder of Islam, in about 570 c.e.
Lazarus Saturday- Orthodox Christian.

APRIL

01. 02:51 ○ Moon Ascending Node,
06:00 ♂ Mars- ♄ Saturn: 0.9° N,
19:12 ○ Moon North Dec.: 23.7° N,
20:21 ◐ First Quarter.
April Fools Day. Veneralia- Festival of Venus, goddess of love and beauty who makes fools of us all. Burn some valerian for Aphrodite on this day to aid love.
Hanuman Jayanti – Hindu.
03. **Esbatd. Pesach-** (Passover) is the main Jewish festival of the year-8 day celebration of the deliverance of the Jews from slavery. A special meal is a central feature.
04. 00:36 ♀ Venus-Pleiades: 0.3° S.
Megalesia – Festival of the Great Mother in honour of the **Magna Mater**, celebrated with processions and games. It derives its name From the Greek meaning to meter; because it also commemorates the books of the Sibylline Oracle brought by King Attalus from Pergama near the temple of this Goddess to Rome.
05. 04:45 ○ Moon-Regulus: 3.9° S.
Lady Luck Day Festival of Fortuna, the goddess of good fortune.
End of Daylight Savings time.
Palm Sunday- Christian.
06. **Manannan's Day** – Celtic.
07. **The Day of Kindly Ones-** Blajini – Kindly spirits are honoured on this day in Romania near natural water sources.
Lord's Evening Meal -Christian.
08. 04:08 ○ Moon Perigee: 356900 km. **Hana-Matsuri-** the festival of **Shaka** the Silent Sage from Japanese Buddhism. Take some time for quiet contemplation with regard to authority figures and family.
09. **Mordron's Day-** Celtic.

Lumeria- the festival in honour of the Lemures, the spirits of dead family members who wander the earth on these three spring nights. The term Lumerians is derived from this festival and is an allegorical word for "Those Long Dead" **Vampires Day-** Christian mutation of Lumeria.
10. **Good Friday.**
12. **Easter Sunday. The Cerealia –** another festival to Ceres. **Festival of Water-** Buddhist statues are washed and then the water is thrown on the followers as a purification ritual.
Baisakhi (Vaisakhi) Sikh.

Celtic Tree Moon of WILLOW

April 15 - May 12 - Gaelic - Saille, (pronounced Sahl-yeh)
The month for rituals associated with healing and growth knowledge, nurturing and women's mysteries.
Willow grows best when there's lots of rain, and in northern Europe there's no shortage of that this time of year. A Willow planted near your home will help ward away danger, floods or storms. They offer protection, and are often found planted near cemeteries. Willows are said to uproot themselves and follow those who walk near them at night.

15. 08:56 ◑ Last Quarter,
19:26 ○ Moon- ♄ Saturn: 2.6° N.
Fordicidia- Festival of the earth goddess Tellus/Gaia - to ensure plenty during the year, and was celebrated under the management of the Vestal Virgins. **The Thesmophoria-** Demeter Hiesmophoria, a surname of Ceres as law-giver, foundress of agriculture and of the civic rite of marriage.
Yom HaShoah- Jewish.
16. 14:33 ○ Moon-4Mars: 2.2° N.
Margo Adler born on this day in 1946. **The Feast Day Of St. Bernadette-** (Christian) at the age of 14, claimed that she had experienced a number of visions of the Virgin Mary. Furthermore, the girl said that the Virgin had imparted miraculous powers of healing to the waters of a spring near a grotto in Lourdes. The Roman Catholic Church declared her visions authentic, and the Lourdes grotto became a shrine for Christian pilgrims though it had been a Pagan sacred site of healing for centuries.
19. **The Cerealia-** festival of Ceres, the grain goddess.
21. 05:01 ○ Moon Apogee: 406500 km. **Festival of Pales-**the Goddess of herds and flocks. It was during the celebration that Romulus built his city.
22. 16:07 Lyrid Shower
Earth Spirit Day- Wiccan - a day to
28. 03:54 ○ Moon Ascending Node. Celtic celebration of the God **Lludd.** work with earth elementals and to perform healing rituals for Gaia.
23. 12:26 ● New Moon.
Saint George's Day- a day to lament the loss of Dragons.
Vinalia festivals, festival to Venus when the wine of the previous year was broached and a libation from it poured on the sod. As goddess of gardens, Venus had vineyards under

her protection. Professional ladies offered her incense of myrtle and mint and bunches of rushes and roses for success in their businesses as well as for beauty, popularity, charm and wit.
The Parilia- Southern Slovenian peasants crown their cows with wreaths of flowers, libations of milk are offered to the Goddess "Pales" from whom we get the term milk-pales. In the evening, the wreaths are fastened to the door of the cattle-stall, where they remain throughout the year.
25. **Anzac Day**. Australia
The Robigalia- festival of the Green Man, God of Growth.
27. 01:23 ○ Moon- ♀ Venus: 6.6° N.
29. 01:23 ○ Moon North Dec.: 23.9° N. **Festival of Flora-** Goddess of fruitfulness and flowers.
30. **Walpurgis Night-** the date of the Pagan festival marking the beginning of summer when the old Pagan witch world was supposed to hold high revelry.
Taliesin Night's (Merlin's night) Celtic celebration of the High priests of Magick. **Death of Alexander Saunders** in 1988, one of the fathers of modern Neo-Wicca.

MAY

01. 06:38 ◐ First Quarter.

✹ Major Sabbat SAMHAIN

in the Southern Hemisphere. Northern Hemisphere **Beltaine, Caileach Beara**, a Celtic Goddess, turns to stone. She is reborn on Samhain. the veil between the wolds thins and with her returns many underworld spirits to the material realm for one night.
Bona Dea (Roman) The festival of Bona Dea, the Roman fertility Goddess. Held on behalf of the public welfare, in the house of the officiating consul or praetor of the city, by matrons and the Vestal Virgins.
02.**Western Wesak-** Visakha Puja-Theravadin Buddhist- anniversary of Buddha's Enlightenment, birth and death. All are said to have occurred during the Taurus full moon (but in Tibet this is not celebrated until the Sagittarius Full Moon in June). Yet the Scorpio full moon in Taurus is magically powerful. Wesak is literally a sacred valley in Tibet to which tens of thousands of people from all around the world travel on a pilgrimage as it is said that the Buddha appears with a company of immortals from Shambhallah, at a table at the end of the valley on Wesak eve to bless humanity. **Vesta** *"Where the sacred fire of the moon is tended by Vestal priestesses, they are usually responsible also for the rain rituals..."* In ancient Rome the Vestal Virgins, guardians of the sacred fire of Vesta, performed a ceremony at the Ides of May, the time of the full moon, to regulate the water supply.
05. 05:21 Eta Aquarid Shower
07:22 ☿ Mercury Superior Conj.
06. 13:03 ○ Moon Perigee: 359700 km.

07. 20:45 ○ Full Moon.
08. **The Festival Of Mens,** the Roman Goddess of mind and consciousness. **Furry Dance Day-** Cornwall- dance in honour of the Horned God to bring good luck to your town.
10. 19:01 ○ Moon Descending Node.
Mothers Day.
11. 16:13 ○ Moon South Dec.: 24° S
12. 19:40 ○ Moon-5Jupiter: 2.4° N.
Cat Parade Day - Belgium. Europeans parade and worship their cats on this day.

Celtic Tree Moon of HAWTHORN

May 13 - June 9
13. 04:18 ○ Moon- ♄ Saturn: 2.8° N.
Fatima - Anniversary of the Goddesses' appearance to 3 children in Fatima in Portugal in 1917.
Bran's Day- Celtic hero's day.
15. 00:03 ◑ Last Quarter,
12:01 ○ Moon-4Mars: 3° N.
The Mercuralia, the festival of Mercury/Hermes, the God of intelligence, magick, communication, merchants and travellers. On this day the merchants sprinkled their heads and their merchandise with water from his well near the Porta Capena.
18. 11:51 ♃ Jupiter- ♄ Saturn: 4.8° N, 17:45 ○ Moon Apogee:405600 km.
20. **Plynteria** – Festival to Athena the goddess of wisdom.
Olwen's Day – Celtic.
21. **Maeve-** the most truly Venusian of the strong Celtic goddesses. It is for her that hawthorn was named May, or May-thorn. She became the goddess of Beltane in whose honour the May queen was crowned. Her most recent name in English lore is Queen Mab in the fairies.
22. 19:37 ☿ Mercury ♀ Venus:0.9° N
23. 03:39 ● New Moon.
Shavuot - Jewish celebration of receiving their "Book Of The Law" from when Moses descended from Mt Sinai with the ten commandments. Plants and flowers are used in decorations.
24. 12:40 ○ Moon-2Venus: 4° N,
20:53 ○ Moon- ♀ Mercury: 3° N.
Birthday of Artemis- (Diana the moon) & her twin brother Helios (Apollo the Sun).
25. 07:34 ○ Moon Ascending Node.
26. 07:16 ○ Moon North Dec.: 24.1° N.
Pentecost – Celebration memorialising the early Christians receiving magical abilities from the Holy Spirit.
30. 13:30 ◐ First Quarter.
Burning Times Remembrance Day- on this day in 1431, Joan of Arc was burned at the stake for the crimes of witchcraft. It is a time to work ritual for religious tolerance and for freedom from dogma and the crimes committed against others by fundamentalists.

JUNE

03. 13:36 ○ Moon Perigee:364400 km
04. 03:42 ♀ Venus Inferior Conj., 22:59 ☿ Mercury Elongation:23.6° E.
06. 05:12 ○ Full Moon,
05:25 ○ Lunar Eclipse.
07. 04:10 ○ Moon Descending Node.
08. 02:22 ○ Moon South Dec.: 24.1° S.
09. 03:19 ○ Moon- ♃ Jupiter: 2.3° N.
12:19 ○ Moon- ♄ Saturn: 2.8° N.

Celtic Tree Moon of OAK

June 10 - July 7 - Gaelic - *Duir*, (meaning "door")
The King Oak rules over the summer months when trees are beginning to reach their full blooming stages. Its Gaelic name is the root word of "Druid" who hold it as the most sacred tree. Used for spells, protection, strength, fertility, money, success, and good fortune. "Knock On Wood" refers to carrying a piece of Oak for good luck. Carry an acorn in your pocket when you go to an interview or business meeting for success. If you catch a falling Oak leaf before it hits the ground, you'll stay healthy the following year.

13. 09:53 ○ Moon- ♂ Mars: 3° N,
16:24 ◐ Last Quarter.
15 10:56 ○ MoonApogee:404600 km
18. ☿ Mercury goes Retrograde in Cancer
19. 18:52 ○ Moon-2Venus: 0.8° S.
20. **The Day of Ceridwen**- sacred to the Celtic Goddess of fertility. Traditionally celebrated in Ireland by tying a ribbon to a tree and making a wish.
Rural Dionysian - Lesser, or Rural, Dionysia, preserved ancient customs centred on a celebration of the first wine. This festival was timed to coincide with the "clearing of the wine", a final stage in the fermentation process occurring in the first cold snap after the Winter Solstice, when it was declared that Dionysus was reborn. Theatrical contest of singing and dancing were performed in his honour.

21. 07:43

✺ **Major Sabbat YULE**

Winter Solstice
The longest night and the shortest day. In the arctic circle the sun misses a day and does not rise. (The No Name Day) The Yule log is burnt to sustain life till the sun (The God Lugh) returns.
14:24 ○ Moon Ascending Node,
16:40 ☼ Annular Solar Eclipse,
16:41 ● New Moon.
Wadjet- the Uracus Goddess, was regarded as governing the eleventh month of the Egyptian year.

CANCER - June 21- July 22

Cardinal sign of ▽ Water - Planetary Ruler ○ Moon.

22. 13:56 ○ Moon North Dec:24.1° N
St. John's Eve- Northern Hemisphere – A Mid-summers magickal herb gathering night. Should be celebrated by us the night after Summer Solstice. A night for gathering and storing herbs as herb are at the height of their magickal properties on this night. See Sabbat notes about this night!
The festival of Fata- the Roman Goddesses of fate and chance.
25. **Ganga Dashami**- Hindu.
26. 00:09 ○ Moon-Regulus: 4.4° S.
28. 18:16 ◑ First Quarter.
30. 12:09 ○ Moon Perigee: 369000 km. **Blodeuwedd's day**- Celtic celebration of beautiful women.

JULY

01. 12:45 ☿ Mercury Inferior Conj.
04. 13:18 ○ Moon Descending Node, 22:59, Aphelion: 1.0167 AU.
05. 11:37 ○ Moon South Dec.: 24.1° S, 14:30 ● Lunar Eclipse,
14:44 ○ Full Moon.
06. 07:37 ○ Moon- ♃ Jupiter: 1.9° N, 18:45 ○ Moon- ♄ Saturn: 2.6° N.
07. **Nonae Caprotinae** ("the nones of the wild fig"), the second festival of Juno, the chief Roman Goddess.
Tanabata or Star Festival (Japan).
Rhea / Cybil Festival Day also sacred to Dionysus.
Anniversary of the Martyrdom of Bab (Baha'i).
08.

Celtic Tree Month of HOLLY

Gaelic: Tinne - pronounced *chihnn-uh*, - July 8- August 4
This evergreen plant reminds us all year long about the immortality of nature and was a potent symbol of masculine energy. The ancients used the wood of the Holly in the construction of weapons. Wear as a charm or hang a sprig of Holly in your house for luck and safety for your family. Make "Holly Water" by soaking leaves overnight in spring water under this full moon to aspire as a blessing or for protection and cleansing.
10. **Holda/Hel Day**- Norse Goddess of the underworld is honoured with black candles and rose petals on this day.
11.**Theano Day**- wife of Pythagoras, "Theano shall contribute the greatness of her intellect".
12. 05:36 ○ Moon- ♂ Mars: 2.2° N.
13. 05:27 ○ Moon Apogee: 404200km, 09:29 ◐ Last Quarter.
14. 17:03 ♃ Jupiter Opposition.
15. **Isis - Osiris' Birthday**. A celebration of the Egyptian Mother Goddess of magick, power, beauty, and love and her twin brother/husband the Egyptian God of fertility, civilisation, agriculture, writing and the underworld, being borne on this day.

The Rosalia - The Roman's feast of roses. The rose was especially sacred to Venus, as goddess of love.
Rosa Mundi - The Rose of the World, the Heart of Creation; the Consuming Fire. The Mother's festival, and is the time that we meditate most deeply upon our relationship to Her. She is the Maker and Shaper of each individual soul in its pure and perfect form. We are born from Her joy, and only in Her are we whole. At the Rosa Mundi rite for the handmaid, everyone is given a rose to hold during the contemplation. The Rose, the grandest, the noblest of Nature's symbols. To the Rosicrucian the Rose was the symbol of Nature, of the ever prolific and virgin Earth, considered as feminine and represented as a virgin woman by the Egyptian initiates, of Isis, the mother and nourisher of man. The altar is decked with roses and candles.
Rath Yatra – Hindu.
17. 17:26 ○ Moon- ♀ Venus: 3.4° S.
18. 22:33 ○ Moon Ascending Node.
19. 21:51 ○ Moon North Dec.: 24.1° N. **Great Panathenala Day One of Six Days** - Every year in the month of Phaophi, the second month of the floods, came the period of eleven days during which the capital celebrated the feast of Opet when Amun and his spouse Mut, the Karnak form of Isis, accompanied by the god Khonsu, proceeded ceremonially at the time of this 'divine emergence', giving the crowd a glimpse of the triad of its three great gods. The telltale number, eleven, points to the festival being the period of 'catching up' the lunar year to the solar by the intercalation of that many days to close the eleven day discrepancy between lunar and solar years. This would originally have been a festival to mark time before the rising of Sirius and the inauguration of the Egyptian New Year. The Nile began to rise at about the same time that the brilliant star Sirius, Sothis, "the Dog Star", after having been invisible for a prolonged period, was first again observed in the sky.
Athena's Day - the birthday of the goddess Athena, the daughter of Métis, the first wife of Zeus. The day of her birth was the day of the beginning of the ancient Greek new-year and was held every fifth year.
Aphrodite - the wedding of Adonis and Aphrodite... There was considerable variation in the date of the festival. In fifth century Athens they were held in April, in Ptolemaic Egypt in September, while under the Empire the accepted date was 19th July.
20. **Egyptian New Year** which is the birthday of Horus; or more accurately when The Dog Star, Sirus, rises in Leo between 6pm and midnight.
21. **Oghma's Day** – Celtic Hercules – He carried a great club but did great deeds via the gift of the gab, and taught the Ogham alphabet to man.
Nana - the lioness, a form of Kybele, appears in the ancient art of India, Mesopotamia, and the Ancient Middle East from 3000 BC up to Classical times.
Damo - Daughter of Pythagoras and

Theano. At his death, Pythagoras entrusted her with all the secrets of his philosophy, and gave her the unlimited care of his compositions.
22. **Neptunalia**, the festival of Neptune, the Roman god of the sea.

22. ♌ **LEO** - July 23 – August 23
Fixed sign of △ Fire-
Planetary Ruler ☼ Sun

24. **Last day of the Great Panathenala** or Egyptian new year festival.
Neith - A feast of lamps was also celebrated at Sais in Egypt in honor of Isis Neith. The ceremony took place in an under-chapel beneath the Temple. Lamps were carried in procession around the coffin of Osiris. 'In Sais the statue of Athena, whom they believe to be Isis, bore the inscription: I am all that has been and is and shall be, and none mortal hath lifted my Veil. In one of the Hermetic texts called "Peplos" (The Veil) it is said that the Veil "signified the Veil of the Universe, studded with stars, the many coloured Veil of Nature, the famous Veil or Robe of Isis, that no mortal has raised". To raise the Veil of Isis means to see Nature as she really is, to understand what it is that underlies the manifestations of this world, and of the emotions which so move us, to see them in their ultimate reality, not veiled any longer... S(he) who is able to do that and so to face reality becomes consciously immortal.
Salacia/Hygia- Goddess of salt & rwater, whose symbol was the pentagram; identified with the Greek Amphitrite, and regarded as the wife of Neptune. This festival is very old.
Hatshepsut- the most famous of the female pharaohs, is honoured for her magick and healing abilities on this day.
25. 14:54 ○ Moon Perigee: 368400 km.
27. 22:32 ◑ First Quarter.
28. 07:08 Delta Aquarid Shower
Pythias- The mother of Pythagoras. He was named after her. She officiated at Delphi as the Pythian oracle.
29. **Guru Purnima/Asadha Purnima**- Hindu.
31. 19:32 ○ Moon Descending Node.

AUGUST

1 ✺ **Major Sabbat: IMBOLC**

The Beginning of Spring – 2nd August or 15 degrees of ♌ Leo in the Southern Hemisphere, or February 2nd or 15 degrees of ♒ Aquarius in the Northern Hemisphere.
IMBOLC (im'molc or im'bolc) means, "in the belly of the mother," or Oimelc means "milk of ewes," for it is also Lambing Season, Candelmas, and Saint Briget's Day. The festival of lights in the southern Hemisphere- Northern Hemisphere Lughnasadh, the Celtic festival marking the harvest period. Also the festival of Lug, the

Celtic hero god**Lughas' Day** - Celtic – God of skill in crafts. A great hero that descends into the underworld to do battle with darkness, his brother on winter solstice (Yule). His body in the underworld was the Yule log. His victorious symbol is the decorated pine tree erected after his return on the 25th. Harvest Games, were held in honour of Lughas from Wales to Lyons.

Macha, Queen of Ireland - the Annual Fair of Macha held at Armagh was established to commemorate Queen Macha of the Golden Hair, who had founded the palace there. The Machas likewise were associated with this feast: The Three Machas are, according to Irish literary tradition, Macha wife of Nemed, Macha wife of Crurmchu and Macha the Red. The third Macha, of the Red, or Golden Hair reigned as Queen of Ireland c.377 BC.

01 18:47 ○ Moon South Dec:24.1° S

02 09:30 ○ Moon- ♃ Jupiter: 1.6° N

02 23:17 ○ Moon- ♄ Saturn: 2.4° N

04. **Culhwch** – Celtic

04 01:59 Full ○ Moon

05

Celtic Tree Month of HAZEL

Gaelic: Coll - August 5 - September 1 translates to "the life force inside you." This is the time of year when Hazelnuts are appearing on the trees, and are an early part of the harvest. Hazelnuts are also associated with wisdom and protection. Hazel is often associated in Celtic lore with sacred wells and magical springs containing the salmon of knowledge. This is a good month to do workings related to wisdom and knowledge, dowsing and divination, and dream journeys. If you're a creative type, such as an artist, writer, or musician, this is a good month to get your muse back, and find inspiration for your talents. Even if you normally don't do so, write a poem or song this month.

07 **The festival of Sol Invictus**, the Roman all conquering Sun god.

Wiccan Festival of Fire Spirits.

Good time to work with the △ fire element.

Chung Yuan - The Hungary Ghost Festival - (blend of Buddhist, Bon, Confucian and Taoist religions) held during the **First ○ Full Moon In August** – This The Chinese are still very partial to keeping the dead happy. They believe that ancestors can influence their joss (luck) in this life. This festival celebrates the time when spirits are let out of purgatory where they never get fed. At midnight, the ghosts must return to purgatory. You can acknowledge these lost souls by leaving bowls of noodles, sweetmeats, cakes and other treats in public places. I highly recommend going to the Chinese quarter of your capital city to enjoy this spectacular festival as lightening the burden of these lost souls can include performances of operas and puppet shows on street corners.

09 17:57 ○ Moon- ♂ Mars: 0.8° N

09 23:51 ○ Moon Apogee:404700 km

10. **Merlins day** - Celtic- today and on the 17th

11. **Puck Fair** a 3-day Irish feast that honours Robin Goodfellow, the famous mischievous sprite.

12 02:45 ◐ Last Quarter

12 23:02Perseid Shower: ZHR = 90

13. **The Vertumnalia**, the festival of Vertumnus, the Roman god of seasons, gardens, and orchards.

Festival of Hecate to be held after dark. The Greeks observed two days sacred to Hecate, one on the 13th of August and one on the 30th of November, whilst the Romans observed the 29th of every month as her sacred day. Hecate was originally a goddess of the wilderness and childbirth originating from Thrace, or among the Carians of Anatolia. Popular cults venerating her as a mother goddess integrated her persona into Greek culture as Ἑκατη. In Ptolemaic Alexandria, she became a goddess of sorcery (which means sister magick) and her role as the 'Queen of Ghosts.' Today she is often seen as a goddess of witchcraft.

13 10:59 ♀ VenusElongation:45.8° W

15.**Festival of Vesta** the Goddess of Hearth Home and health celebrate her by lighting a sacred flame to her today.

Festival of Torches to Diana - Her chief festival. Her groves shone with a multitude of torches.

Funadama matsuri (Japanese) On August 15 at the Hodosan jinja, Saitama, the Funadama matsuri ("boat festival") is held. This festival dates from the Tokugawa period when travellers by raft from Chichibu to Eda prayed for safe passage on the Arakawa River.

Teej – Hindu - has become Indian Independence Day

15 05:22 ○ Moon Ascending Node

15 23:01 ○ Moon- ♀ Venus: 4.2° S

16 06:40 ○ Moon North Dec.: 24.2° N

17.**The Portunalia**, the festival of Portunes, the Roman god of gates, doors, and harbours. At this festival, people would throw keys into the fire in order to bless them.

18 00:47 ☿ Mercury Superior Conj.

19. **The Vinalia**, the festival of Venus and Minerva, at that time temples and gardens were set apart for her, and then the kitchen gardeners went on holiday. An old Vinalia invocation:- "I beseech Minerva and Venus, of whom the one protects the olive yard, and the other the garden and in her honour the rustic Vinalia has been established."

Raksha Bandhan- Humanity Day- (Hindu)

19 12:41● New Moon

20. **The Festival Of Consus**, the Roman god of good council.

21 20:59 ○ Moon Perigee: 363500 km

23. **The Volcanalia**, the festival of Vulcan, the Roman god of fire. This took place during the height of the Mediterranean drought and the period of highest risk of fire. On the banks of the river Tiber, fires were lighted on which living fish were sacrificed.

Genia (Genie, Genius – Higher Self) of Personal Fate. The threads of Moira draw all things in life together. Her particular symbols are the wheel and the scales. This day is especially one for examining the direction of one's soul and making resolutions for the future.

Nemesia - in memory of deceased persons. The Goddess Nemesis was supposed to defend the relics and memory of the dead from all insult.

♍ VIRGO 24 Aug – 23 Sept

Mutable sign of ▽ Earth -

Planetary Ruler ☿ Mercury.

25. **Ops** - Abundance. Consivia was the old Italian Goddess of fertility, sowing and reaping. Only the Vestals and one of the pontifices could attend. Her abode was in the earth, so her worshipers invoked her while seated and touching the ground.

Onam – Hindu.

26. **Luonnotar** – A Finnish Goddess, or the Water Mother, was the Creatrix of the World. Upon her knees the duck laid the six golden and the one iron egg from which the world was made.

26 03:58 ◑ First Quarter

26 14:05 ○ Moon-Antares: 6.4° S

27 21:52 ○ Moon Descending Node

28. **Raksha-Bandhan**- Hindu

29 00:06 ○ Moon South Dec.: 24.2° S

29 11:33 ○ Moon-5Jupiter: 1.5° N

30. 02:40 ○ Moon- ♄ Saturn: 2.3° N

31. **Hathor** – Her birthday, Thoth 1, was the beginning of the New Year on the fixed Alexandrian Calendar. Before dawn the priestesses would bring Hathor's image out onto the terrace to expose it to the rays of the rising sun, followed by ladies cracking mystic whips, crowned with flowers and leading a drunken carnival.

SEPTEMBER

2 The Celtic Tree Moon of VINE

Gaelic: Muinn - September 2 - September 29

a time of great harvest from the grapes of the Mediterranean to the fruits of the northern regions, the Vine produces fruits we can use to make that most wondrous concoction called wine.The Vine is the symbol of creeping sensuality and entangling emotions. A hardy, long-lived plant. It's symbol, the white swan represents the white ghosts or the white phantom, Gwenhwyvar. The equinox is a time when for a brief moment all is in balance. The light and the dark hold equal positions, the balance of the mundane and the supernatural; the mortal and the immortal. This Ogham represents the letter M in the Tree Alphabet as well as Muinn in the Calendar. Vine is "The whispered words of sweet poetry."

02 15:22 Full ○ Moon

03. **Viking 2 Mars Landing** 1976.

04.**The Celtic Feast of Rhiannon**

Krishna Janmashtami Krishna took birth at midnight on the ashtami or the 8th day of the Krishnapaksha or dark fortnight in the Hindu month of Shravan (August-September). This auspicious day is called **Janmashthami**. - Hindu.

Geronimo Surrendered 1886.

05. **Shikshak Divas.**

Teacher's Day.

06. **Father's Day.**

06 14:42 ○ Moon- ♂ Mars: 0°

06 16:31 ○ Moon Apogee: 405600 km

07. **National Threatened Species Day.**

Healer's Day - Wiccan – A day to honour all forms of healers and to do a ritual requesting healing.

The Greek Feast of Asclepigenaia -An Eleusinian Priestess.

Mao Tse-Tung died 1976

10 19:26 ◐ Last Quarter

11. **The Matriarchy of Egypt**

All Queens were High Priestesses of Egypt, and Initiates of the Inner Mysteries. Their power was hidden, but it was they who ruled Egypt through the Pharoah of the time, whether he was their brother, husband or father. No man could become Pharoah (the Living Horus, the resurrected Osiris) other than by marriage to such a Lady of the Royal Line which ran through the female side, and derived ultimately from Isis.

Padmasambhava Day –Tibetan Buddhist.

Ethiopian New Year's Day – Rastafarian.

11 09:05 ○ Moon Ascending Node

12. **Hildegard of Bingen** (1098-1179) – One of the first campaigners of women's rights against the Catholic Church from within the Celtic Church in Germany. She wrote over a hundred letters on this subject to emperors, popes, bishops, archbishops, nuns and the nobility, as well as seventy poems and nine books describing her visions of the universe, dictated to her secretary, Monk Volmar. In her own words, "When I was forty-two years and seven months old, a burning light of tremendous brightness coming from heaven poured into my entire mind. Like a flame that does not burn but enkindles, it inflamed my entire heart and my entire breast, just like the sun that warms an object with its rays... All of a sudden, I was able to taste of the understanding of the narration of books. ...". In a letter to Abbot Adam of Ebrach, Hildegard reported seeing in a vision "an extraordinarily beautiful Young Woman wearing shoes which seemed of purest gold whom the whole creation called-Lady". The image spoke to a female human of sapphire blue and said: "Dominion is yours on the day of your power in the radiance of the saints. I have brought you forth from my own womb before the daystar. (♀ Venus)" Then Hildegard heard a voice tell her, "The young woman whom you see is Love. She has her tent in Eternity... For it was Love which was the source of this creation in the beginning…". Hildegard asked, "Why does the whole Creation call this maiden "Lady?" She received the reply: "Because it was from Her that all creation proceeded, since Love as the First. She made everything".In Hildegard's writing and her illuminations one can see influences

of the ancient Goddess religions, of the Roman Aurora, The Egyptian Isis, the old Germanic Horsel, and the Hebrew Hokma.

12 15:25 ☉ Moon North Dec:24.4° N
13. **Ramadan Begins** Muslim.
Egyptian Day Of The Dead – On this day ancient Egyptians lit fires to honour the dead and the Goddess Nephthys.
Rosh Hashanah/Jewish New Year -13-14 September.
13 14:50 ☉ Moon-Pollux: 4.5° N
14 14:43 ☉ Moon-♀ Venus: 4.6° S
15. **Ganesh/Vinayak Chaturthi**
Ganesha — the festival to celebrate and glorify the elephant-deity riding a mouse. A clay model of Lord Ganesha is made 2-3 months prior to the day of Ganesh Chaturthi. On the day of the festival, it is placed on raised platforms in homes. The priest invokes life into the idol.
17. **Astraea / Dike / Virgo**
The Greeks call Virgo Dike or Justitia), because she is thought to hold the neighboring Scales (♎Libra).
It is fabled that The Starry Goddess, Astraea, returned in the iron age as the impersonation of Justice, whose symbol was the Scales, to praise equity. "She dwelt on earth and met men face to face, nor ever disdained in olden time the tribes of men and women, but mingling with them took her seat, immortal though she was. Her, men called Justice (Dike)... Nor yet in that age had men knowledge of hateful strife... Even so long as the earth nurtured the Golden Age, she had her dwelling on earth... Yet in that Silver Age was she still upon the earth, but from the echoing hills at eventide she came alone. But when they, too, were dead, and when, more ruinous than they which went before, the Race of Bronze was born, who were the first to forge the sword of the highwayman, and the first to eat the flesh of the ploughing-ox, then verily did Justice loathe that race of men and fly heavenward and took up that abode, where even now in the night-time the Maiden (Virgo) is seen...". (Aratus, Phaenomena) Upholder of Justice: Trump VIII of Tarot.
Maat - Goddess who protects Truth with her outstretched wings. She sits on the fulcrum of the scales that balance the deeds of the heart against her one white feather.
17 21:00 ●New Moon
18. **Luang Phor Sodh attained Dhammakaya** (lunar) Thai Buddhist.
18 23:44 ☉ Moon Perigee: 359100 km
19. **The Fast of Thoth**, this day long fast honors the Egyptian god of wisdom and magic.
Lailat - Ul - Bara'h - The Night of Forgiveness- Muslim.
City Dionysia – were the main festivities for the God Dionysus, as well as being an urban carnival or Komos. They were held around the time of the Spring Equinox, about three months after the Rural Dionysia, to celebrate the end of winter and the arrival of the new vine-growing season. It was celebrated with a great drama festival. Dionysus was also the god of acting, music, and poetic inspiration. Tragedy plays were more important than comedy at this festival. The prize for the winner of the tragedy festival was a goat, (the Greek word for goat is the origin of the word "tragedy") a common symbol of Dionysus, and his tragic early life.
20. **Luang Phor** Sodh attained Dhammakaya (solar) Thai Buddhist
22 23:31 **Autumnal Equinox**

❋ **Major Sabbat OSTRA**

The Festival of The Sacred Egg of new life. The Goddess Ostra returns to the earth seeding all things with fertility.
23 22:33 ☉ Moon Descending Node
24 11:55 ☽ First Quarter
25 05:11 ☉ Moon South Dec:24.5° S
25 16:46 ☉ Moon-5Jupiter: 1.7° N
26 06:46 ☉ Moon-6Saturn: 2.5° N
30

The Celtic Tree Moon of IVY

Gaelic *Gort*, pronounced *go-ert*.
September 30 - October 27
As the year comes to a close and Samhain approaches, the Ivy moon rolls in at the end of the harvest season. Ivy often lives on after its host plant has died, a reminder to us that life goes on, in the endless cycle of life, death and rebirth. Ivy protects the home it grow upon. This is a time to banish the negative from your life. Do workings related to improving yourself, and placing a barricade between you and the things that are toxic to you. Ivy can be used in magic performed for healing, protection, cooperation, and to bind lovers together.
30 **Greater Eleusinian Mysteries**
Day Eight of Nine Days
On the eighth day the Lesser Mysteries were repeated.

OCTOBER

1. **Greater Eleusinian Mysteries – Day Nine of Nine Days**
The last day of the Great Mysteries at Eleusis was devoted to plenty in its liquid form. This was the day of the plemochoai, 'the pourings of plenty'. So called, also, were the two unstable circular vases that were set up for this ceremony... The plemochoai were poured into a cleft in the earth... one vessel was set up in the east, the other on the west side, and both overturned. The liquid with which they had been filled is not named. (Kerenyi, Eleusis.)
The Celtic Tree Calendar Month IVY - Gaelic: Gort - October 1 - October 28
In contrast to the Vine, Ivy is evergreen, and it represents the immortal spirit. The Celts associate Ivy with their lunar goddess Arianrhod, and their ritual to her marked the opening of the portal to the fairy worlds through the dark side of the moon. The Butterfly is their symbol. Ivy represents mysterious and the mystical spiritual worlds. This Ogham represents the letter G in the Tree Alphabet as well as Gort in the Calendar. The Ivy is "The Wild Boar of ruthless hunt."
The Festival Of Fides, the Roman Goddess of good faith, honesty, and oaths.
Guiding Spirits Day – Wiccan festival to guardian and guiding spirits celebrated by light a candle on the altar or a blazing fir in the home fireplace.
2. **Gandhi Jayanti.** Birthday of Mahatma Gandhi (1869 - 1948), India's "Father of the Nation.
02 01:59 ☿ Mercury Elongation: 25.8° E
02 07:05 Full ☉ Moon
3. **The Festival Of Dionysus**, the Greek god of wine and revelry, also known as Bacchus to the Romans.
03 13:21 ☉ Moon- ♂ Mars: 0.8° N
4. **Celtic Feast day of Pwyll.** Pwyll, the Celtic ruler of the Otherworld, was given 'The Stone,' one of four treasures given to him for safekeeping. The Stone represents the right of the Kings and Queens to have divine power.
04 03:22 ☉ Moon Apogee:406300 km
6. **Daylight Savings Starts-** Australia
7. **World Animal Day**
08 10:29 ☉ Moon Ascending Node
9. **The Festival Of Felicitas**, the Roman Goddess of good luck and joy.
09 23:07 ☉ Moon North Dec:24.6° N
Birthday of Luang Phor Sodh (solar) – Thai Buddhist
10 10:39 ☽ Last Quarter
11. **Pitr-Paksha ends / Mahalaya** is an auspicious occasion observed seven days before the Durga Puja, and heralds the advent of Durga, the goddess of supreme power. It is an invocation or invitation to the mother goddess to descend on earth - "Jago Tumi Jago."
Thanksgiving Day (Canada)
The Meditrinalia, the festival of Meditrina, the Roman Goddess of healing, wine, and health.
12. **Navaratri** begins. Literally the nine nights invokes the energy aspect of the universal mother, commonly referred to as "Durga," which literally means the remover of miseries of life. She is also referred to as "Devi" (goddess) or "Shakti" (energy or power). God is motionless, absolutely changeless, and the Divine Mother Durga, does everything.
Birthday of Alistair Crowley-on this day in 1875.
The Festival Of Fortuna Redux, the Roman Goddess of successful journeys and safe returns from those journeys.
Our Lady of Fatima. The last appearance of the Virgin Mary at Fatima took place on 13 October 1917.
The Greater Eleusinian Mystery was, I believe, manifested at Fatima. Here we have people seeing a Golden Disc bringing from the sky the apparition of a woman robed in white. The visions were shown to three children, and occurred on each thirteenth of the month, from May to October; so including the ancient dates of the Mysteries of the Goddesses. At the culmination in October, seventy thousand onlookers saw a sun disc revolve and show spectroscopic change; they called it 'the dancing sun'. (Olivia Robertson, The Call of Isis, p125) 'It is already time that each one of us accomplishes holy deeds of his own initiative and reforms his own life..."
Eid Al Fitr End Of Ramadan - Muslim
13. 21:08 ○ FULL MOON
The Festival Of Fontus, the Roman god of springs.
14 Mercury goes Retrograde in Scorpio
14 09:10 ♂ Mars Opposition
14 09:57 ☉ Moon- ♀ Venus: 4.4° S
15. **St Teresa of Avila** Saint of the Ecstatic Orgasm – Born October 15 1515 and died October 15 1582.
Pandrosus- The first priestess of Athena.
18. **Durga Puja (Maha Saptami)** Twice a year, close to our major Sabbats of the at the cross quarters, Hindus observe nine days of ceremonies, rituals, fasts and feasts in honour of the supreme mother goddess Durga and her aspects of Lakshmi and Saraswati – 3 days for each. 6 days after the commencements is Durga's big day!
End of Buddhist Lent – Thai Buddhist
Drawing Down the Sun – Gardinerian Wicca – The priest of a coven perform a ceremony in honour of the horned god of fertility and wild animals
17 05:31 ●New Moon
17 09:46 ☉ Moon Perigee:356900 km
19. **Dhak Bad Tewo Devorohana**, at 9:00 a.m. "Coming down from the deva world", a special alms round circling the main temple building, in memory of the return of the Buddha from Tavatimsa or second heaven, after proclaiming the Dhamma to his mother in order to repay her kindness. Thai Buddhist
The Armilustrium, the second festival of Mars, the Roman god of war. On this day, military arms were ritually purified and put in storage for winter.
20. 04:00 ☿ Mercury at Greatest Elong: 25°E
Navaratri ends
Birthday of the Bab -Baha'i
21. **Selket**- The Egyptian sky-diagram, first found on a coffin-fragment excavated at Asyut of about 2050 BC shows above the Lion a Scorpio Goddess, identifiable with the Babylonian goddess Ishhara. Selket heralded the sunrise through her temples at the autumn equinox about 3700-3500 BC and was the symbol of Isis in the pyramid ceremonials.
Ishhara- Scorpio was known to the Babylonians as the female scorpion Ishhara, the wife of the Archer.
Demeter- The month for sowing, in the season of the Plciades, the Egyptians call Athyr (sacred to Hathor), the Athenians Pyanepsion and the Bcoeotians Damatrios, 'the month sacred to Demeter'.

The Celtic Feast Day of Cerridwen
Vijaya Dashami/ Dusshera or Vijayadashami- This occurs on the "tenth" day following the Navratri. It is a festival to celebrate the triumph of good over evil, and marks the defeat and death of the demon king Ravana in the epic Ramayana. Huge effigies of Ravana are burnt amidst the bangs and booms of firecrackers.

21 01:53 ○ Moon Descending Node
21 15:21 Orionid Shower: ZHR = 20
22. **Labour Day** NZ
22 12:00 ○ Moon South Dec:24.7° S
23 03:10 ○ Moon- ♃ Jupiter: 2.1° N
23 13:49 ○ Moon- ♄ Saturn: 2.7° N
23 23:23 ◑ First Quarter

♏SCORPIO Oct 24 – Nov 22
Fixed Sign of 🜄 Water-
Planetary Ruler ♇ Pluto

24 **Birthday of Luang Phor Sodh** (lunar) Thai Buddhist.
United Nations Day
Spirits of the Air Day – Wiccan day of incense offering to the air elementals.
25. **Lakshmi Puja / Sharad Purnima-** On the full moon night following Dusshera or Durga Puja, Hindus worship Lakshmi ceremonially at home, pray for her blessings, and invite neighbours to attend the Puja. It is believed that on this full moon night the goddess herself visits the homes and replenishes the inhabitants with wealth. A special worship is also offered to Lakshmi on the auspicious Diwali night

26 04:14 ☿ Mercury Inferior Conj

28 **The Celtic Tree Moon of REED**

Gaelic: Ngetal - Oct 28 – Nov 23
Identified with what is submerged or hidden, the reed represents the mysteries of death. The Fire Feast of Samhain this month celebrates the dead and the boundary between the worlds thinning, thus it represents the hidden roots to all life. The Reed is associated with a saviour and a custodian. The Reed is also the symbol of Royalty. The White Hounds represent the dogs that guard the lunar mysteries. There is no translation or letter usage of Ngetal in the Celtic Tree Alphabet. Reed is "The restless noise of the wine dark sea"
Karwa Chauth: Fast for Married Women- A ritual of fasting observed by married Hindu women seeking the longevity, well-being, and prosperity of their husbands. All wives expect lavish gifts from their husbands! Unmarried women, widows, and spinsters are barred from observing this fast. No food or water can be taken after sunrise. Shiva, Parvati and their son Kartikeya are worshipped on this day along with the 10 'karwas' (earthen pots) filled with sweets. The Karwas are given to daughters, sisters and female friends along with gifts. At night when the moon appears, women break their fast after offering water to the moon. In the evening, the fasted women party, feast, and dress up in special clothes, usually a red or pink sari, jewellery, with 'mehendi' or henna patterns on the hands and decorative 'bindis' on the forehead. The fasted women from all over the neighbourhood gather in a group and narrate mythological stories that underscore the significance of Karwa Chauth. This festival comes 9 days before Diwali on 'kartik ki chauth', i.e., on the fourth day of the new moon immediately after Dusshera, in the month of 'Karthik' (October-November). 'Chauth' means the 'fourth day' and 'Karwa' is an earthen pot with a spout - a symbol of peace and prosperity - that is necessary for the rituals.
31.**Kathin** - During the month following Ok Phansa, between the full moons of October and November. New robes will be offered to the monks on that day. – Thai Buddhist
Lailat- Ul- Qadr- The Night of Power- Muslim
Beltane Major |Solar Sabbat 31st Oct to 1st Nov is when **Beltane** is celebrated in the southern hemisphere see "This Season Sabbats" for more Beltane details. – **Samhain Eve** - Northern Hemisphere – **Day One of Three Days**
The Goddess Samhain- The Goddess of the first day of winter. Several Irish authors derive the name Samhain from the Semitic word Shamiyim, or with the Phoenician Samen, meaning "Heaven." "Red Hanrahan on Samhain Night came to the point where he could walk no longer, so sat down on the heather where he was, in the heart of Slieve Echtge. And after a while he took notice that there was a door close to him, and a light coming from it, and he wondered that being so close to him he had not seen it before. And he rose up and, tired as he was, went in at the door, and although it was night-time outside, it was daylight he found within. And presently he met with an old man that had been gathering summer thyme and yellow flagflowers, and it seemed as if all the sweet smells of summer were with him. And with that he brought him into a very big shining house, and every grand thing that Hanrahan had ever heard of, and every colour he had ever seen, was in it. There was a high place at the end of the house, and on it there was sitting in a high chair a woman, the most beautiful the world ever saw, having a blond pale face and flowers about it, but she had the tired look of one that had been long waiting. And there were sitting on the step below her chair four grey old women, and the one of them was holding a great cauldron in her lap; and another a great stone upon her knees, and heavy as it was it seemed light to her; and another of them had a very long spear that was made of pointed wood; and the last of them had a sword that was without a scabbard. Then the first of the old women rose up, holding the cauldron between her two hands, and she said, 'Pleasure'; then the second old woman rose up with the stone in her arms and she said, Tower'; and the third old woman rose up with a spear in her hand, and she said, 'Courage'; and the last of the old women rose up having the sword in her hands, and she said, 'Knowledge'. And then the four old women went out of the door bringing their four treasures with them. (Yeats, Mythologies, p220.)
All-Hallows, is the feast of the dead in Pagan and Christian times, signalising the close of harvest and the initiation of the winter season, lasting until May. Hallowe'en was perhaps of old the most important feast, since the Celts would seem to have dated the beginning of the year from it rather than Beltane. In ancient Ireland, a new fire used to be kindled every year on Hallowe'en on the Eve of Samhain, and from this sacred flame all the fires in Ireland were kindled. Such a custom points strongly to Samhain (the first of November) as New Year's Day. The fairies (the sidhe pronounced the shay) were imagined as particularly active at this season, from which the half-year is reckoned. The Ultonians held of the fair of Samhain in the plain of Murthemne (County Louth) every year: and nothing whatever was done by them during that time but games and races, pleasure and amusement, and feasting: and it is from this circumstance that the Trenae Samna (three days of Sarnhain) are still observed throughout Ireland. All Celtic feasts begin in the evening at sundown about 6pm which was the start of the next day (Not midnight)... its activities still mark Hallowe'en as one of the great 'spirit nights' of the Celtic peoples. On this evening the living reached out to the souls of the dead whilst the veil between the worlds was the thinnest. Families sat up till midnight and little cakes, known as Soul Cakes, were eaten by everyone. There were still a few children in 1938, going from door to door 'souling' for cakes or money by singing a song. As the clock struck twelve there was silence, for at this hour the souls of the dead would revisit their earthly homes. There were candles burning in every room to guide them. and there was a glass of wine on the table to refresh them.
Tlachtga- also had a feast dedicated to her. The Fire Festivals are distinctly Female in nature. Samhain is the festival of Hecate, the Old Moon Goddess. The eight local mother goddesses of Ireland were then the patrons of the great seasonal feasts and assemblies. King Tuathal Teachtrnhar in the year 79 built the royal scat of Tlachtga, where the fire Tlachtga was ordained to be kindled. The use of this sacred fire was to summon the priests, augurs and druids of Ireland to repair thither and assemble upon the eve of All Saints. No other fire should be kindled upon that night throughout the kingdom, so that the fire that was to be used in the country was to be derived from this holy fire.
The Isia – Day One of Four Days- Isis, like Demeter, had two great festivals, one in the spring and another in the autumn. The autumnal celebration consisted of a passion play which continued for four days – although the date varied in different places, it usually began on October 31st and ended on November 3rd. Actors impersonating Isis, Nephthys, Anubis, Horus, searched for the body of Osiris. They shrouded the gilded image of a cow with a black linen as a sign of the Goddess in mourning, they lead the black-veiled golden cow seven times round the temple of Helios and this perambulation is called the seeking for Osiris.' Unlike The Elusian mysteries it was not conducted in strict secrecy, for it was a public out doors performance and pageant of the resurrection of Osiris by Isis. "Come to thy house, O fair youth, that thou mayest see me. I am thy sister, whom thou lovest; thou shalt not part from me. Yet, doth my heart yearn after thee and mine eyes desire thee. Come to her who loves thee, Come to thy sister, come to thy Wife, thou shalt not be far from me. I call after thee and weep my brother, my brother." (A Lament of Isis from the play.) The most stirring and most suggestive, incorporating a sex act, was the commemoration of the Finding of Osiris and the reassembling him. The 14th part his penis was missing so Isis made an artificial one, had sex with it and conceived Horus. This festival was held at Abydos and and at Rome at the beginning of each November.
Bau/Gula
In the old days of Gudea of Lagash the year commenced with the festival of the Goddess Bau in the middle of October; in the later Babylon of Hammurabi the feast was transferred to the spring, and the first month of the year began in March. However, the older calendar of Babylonia had been already carried to the West. The ancient Canaanite year began in the autumn in what the later calendar reckoned the seventh month. The festal calendar of Lagash going back to Sumerian times is well known. There the New Year Festival was celebrated with the marriage of the goddess Bau to the god Ningirsu.
Gwydion the Dagda
The day of his awakening and magickal empowerment
Rebirth of Caileach Beara, the Celtic Goddess who turned to stone on May 1 (Beltane).

30 02:13 ○ Moon- ♂ Mars: 3.3° N
31 04:46 ○ MoonApogee:406400 km

NOVEMBER

1. ❂ **Major Sabbat BELTANE**

Pagan Fertility Celebrations for the coming of summer.
Day of the Dead in most South American and Mexican cultures. Offerings of food and strong drink are offered to the spirits of the deceased.
Divali –Sikh
Isia – Day Two of Four Days
Samhain – Day Two of Three Days
Tea- The Assembly of Tara, the ancient religious and political centre of Ireland, was under the patronage of the goddess Tea, and took place on

Samhain. Today this ancient site is being destroyed to make way for a freeway. There is a tradition in early Irish legends of holding the sacred feast of Samhain on the shores of lakes. In the story of 'The Dream of Angus', the feast is held by the side of Loch Bel Dracon by swan-girls, symbolic of otherworldly souls, wearing magic necklets.

All Saints- The Christian Churchs celebrates the presence of All Saints and All Souls following the vigil of All Souls' Eve by tending and tiding the grave plots in the local cemetery.

Celtic Feast Day if - Lly

2. Isia - Day Three of Four Days

Samhain – Day Three of Three Days- On the third day of the Seeking of Osiris the celebrants 'go down to the sea at night-time; and the keepers of the robes and the priests bring forth the hallowed chest containing a small golden coffer, into which they pour some drinkable water which they have taken up, and a great shout arises from the company for joy that Osiris is found. Then they knead some fertile soil with the water and mix in spices and incense of a very costly sort, and fashion there from a crescent-shaped figure which they clothe and adorn.' (Plutarch, De Iside et Osiride)

All Souls' Day- The feast of All Saints on November 1st was instituted in the ninth century, and the feast of All Souls' Day on November 2nd in 998 AD

Anniversary of the Crowning of Haile Selassie - Rastafarian

Dance of the Fiery Stars - a Dionysus ritual

01 00:49 Full ○ Moon

3. Gaelic New Year's Day

Melbourne Cup Day

Isia – Day Four of Four Days (The Hilaria)- Then Isis fanned the cold clay with her wings, breathed her own life into the nostrils of Osiris and with the help of spells from Thoth accomplished the resurrection of Osiris to a second and eternal life. As he lay there reconstituted, she fluttered over his erect phallus in the form of a white kite and conceived the golden falcon, Horus, who was to avenge the death of his father. This day was marked in the Roman calendar with the name Hilaria, because the crowd shouted for joy, 'Osiris has been found!' The celebrants were given over to the most unrestrained rejoicing, since the God, now risen to immortality, would assess all who had become divine by drinking the milk of Isis.

04 12:39 ○ Moon Ascending Node
05 15:50 South Taurid Shower:ZHR=1
06 05:30 ○ Moon North Dec:24.8° N
08 23:46 ☽ Last Quarter
09. Diwali — the Festival of Lights! Day One

Durga Puja - Kali Puja in Bengal
Is a four-day celebration that is the biggest of all Hindu festivals as the celebration of life, its enjoyment and goodness. Every household cleans their houses and lights up candles all over their houses. Children and adults set off firecrackers all night. No one sleeps on first night. Durga/Kali is honoured as representing feminine strength, motherly love and dynamic energy that mocks human ignorance. Mythology says that Shiva and Kali are the originating couple of the universe but Kali even mocks Shiva, as if she herself is the unique source of everything. In reflection during this celebration, all women are honoured as mothers and sisters and given sweets. Begin and end this celebration by ritually cleansing your self and your home. Light a candle, sit quietly, shut your eyes, withdraw the senses, concentrate on this supreme light that illuminates the soul. Originally a harvest festival it is linked the worship of Mother Kali, the celebration of the marriage of Lakshmi with Lord Vishnu, Ganesha, and commemorates the return of Lord Rama along with Sita and Lakshman from his fourteen year long exile and vanquishing the demon-king Ravana. In Jainism, it is the great event of Lord Mahavira attaining the eternal bliss of nirvana. All celebrated with lights and firecrackers on each night. It is believed that on this day, Goddess Parvati played dice with her husband Lord Shiva, and she decreed that whosoever gambled on Diwali night would prosper throughout the ensuing year. The first day of the festival Naraka Chaturdasi marks the vanquishing of the demon Naraka by Lord Krishna and his wife Satyabhama.

10. Celtic Feast day of – Arawen
Diwali — the Festival of Lights!
Day Two - Amavasya,
The second day of Deepawali, marks the worship of Lakshmi, the Goddess of wealth, in her most benevolent mood, fulfilling the wishes of her devotees.

Reason- On November 10th 1793 a festival was held in Notre Dame de Paris in honour of 'Reason and Liberty,' represented by women. Mlle Candeille wore a red Phrygian cap, a white frock, a blue mantle, and tricolour ribbons. Her head was filleted with oak-leaves **The Festival Of Fontus**, the Roman god of springs.. In the cathedral a sort of 'Temple of Philosophy' was erected on a mound, and in this temple Mlle Candeille was installed. Young girls crowned with oak-leaves were her attendants, and sang hymns in her honour.

Kali Puja- Special rituals to Kali on the 2nd day of the Diwali

11. Diwali — the Festival of Lights!
Day Three - Kartika Shudda Padyami
The third day of Deepawali that Bali steps out of hell and rules the earth according to the boon given by Lord Vishnu, who in his dwarf incarnation vanquished the tyrant Bali, and banished him to hell. Bali was allowed to return to earth once a year, to light millions of lamps to dispel the darkness and ignorance, and spread the radiance of love and wisdom. On the 3rd day a white-buffalo is offered to the Goddess, so you may leave her a small offering of bull or buffalo meat before her image on your personal altar

11 02:59 ☿ Mercury Elongation:19.1° W

12. Diwali — the Festival of Lights! Day Four - Yama Dvitiya /Bhai Dooj
On the fourth day of Deepawali, sisters invite their brothers to their homes, ritualise their love by putting an auspicious tilak or a vermilion mark on the forehead of their brothers, and perform an aarti of him by showing him the light of the holy flame as a mark of love and protection from evil forces. Sisters are lavished with gifts, goodies, and blessings from their brothers.

Ascension of 'Abdu'l-Bahá - Baha'i -
Anniversary of the Birth of Baha'u'llah - Baha'i -

12 15:06 NorthTauridShower:ZHR=15
13 07:31 ○ Moon- ♀ Venus: 3° S
14 21:48 ○ Moon Perigee: 357800 km
15 15:07 ● New Moon
16. Sangha Day – Buddhist –
22. St Cecilia - A Roman lady of the third century, patroness of music, and of the blind.
Thanksgiving – Interfaith
17 10:07 ○ Moon Descending Node
17 21:24 Leonid Shower: ZHR = 15
18 21:27 ○ Moon South Dec:24.9° S
19 18:54 ○ Moon- ♃ Jupiter: 2.6° N
20 00:57 ○ Moon- ♄ Saturn: 3° N
22 14:45 ☽ First Quarter

♐ **SAGITTARIUS-** Nov 23 – Dec 22
Mutable Sign of △ Fire -
Planetary Ruler ♃ Jupiter

23. Artemis/Diana- The Romans assigned the virgin Goddess of hunting and the moon, Diana, to Sagittarius. The month of Sagittarius is a sacred time to the Goddesses of Menstruation.

Ishtar
In Babylon, the Sabbatu of the moon-goddess was at the full moon, and it was then that she was thought to be menstruating. Women who live closely together will often come to menstruate simultaneously. That is why menstruation has often been called The Wise Wound. It is therefore possible that her colleges of priestesses menstruated in synchrony with each other and in sympathy with the Moon. The Sabbaths of the Jews were closely related in their origin to the Babylonian Sabbaths, but it is strange to us to think that the prohibitions connected with 'Sabbath observance' are, in their far-off origins, menstrual taboos connected with the belief that the moon is herself a woman having a monthly period. 'Menstruation' literally means 'moon-change.' In Babylon, the two most important points of the Moon's course, from the religious point of view, were the full moon (shabattum), and the day of the moon's total disappearance (bubbulum). The latter was marked by fasting, prayers, and other rites.

Hathor
The goddess Hathor, the Venus of the Egyptians presided over the Western quarter of Thebes. It was into her arms that the sun sinking behind the mountain, was poetically supposed to be received, and in this character answered also to Night.

Al,Uzzah
'The Great One', the Arabian Venus lies behind the Muslim holy day, which is Friday, always considered a lucky day for marriage. The colours of Muslim flags unconsciously honour the female element in displaying the green, or the vert, or the woman's colour, or Friday colour, that of the Muslim Sabbath. This green is that of the Venus of Mecca.

Freya
Freya was esteemed the mother of all the gods. She was worshipped as the goddess of love and pleasure, who bestowed on her votaries a variety of delights, particularly happy marriage, and easy childbirths. To Freya the sixth day of the week was consecrated, which still bears her name, Friday.

Shekinah
Shekinah, the magickal light over the ark of the covenant was thought to embody the form of a divine queen and bride, who joined them every Friday at dusk to bring them joy and happiness on the Sacred Sabbath meal. According to Raphael Patai 'Sabbath' is the name of the Goddess who is the consort of the Jewish God. Just as in Tantric Hinduism, so Jehovah had his lover, Sabbath. Often confused with Shekinah who, to this day, in every Jewish temple or synagogue she is welcomed in the Friday evening prayers with the words, 'Come, O bride! Friday night, the Eve of the Sabbath, is the time when man comes together with his wife and the Shekinah fills the house. The Sabbath itself, Saturday, is kept holy and no masculine business venture or work is undertaken, in the Goddess's holy afterglow of loving intercourse between man and woman. Torah scholars perform marital intercourse precisely on Friday night for the reason that the earthly union was symbolic of the heavenly marriage between Jehovah and his Bride, Sabbath or Sacred Seventh, which generates Shekinah. The Hebrew tribes who originally worshipped Ashera, Ashteroth and Astart-Anath by pouring out libations to the Queen of Heaven as the modern Jews do every Friday.

The Virgin Mary
She is called by orthodox Catholic Fathers, The Moon of the Church, Our Moon, Spiritual Moon, The Perfect and Eternal Moon...

Manat/Allaat
Manat was the Arabian Goddess of the Moon, and when combined with the powers of Venus was known as Allaat - spelt in exactly the same way as the present Arabic word for God, Allaah. The Goddess is implicitly the foundation of Islam, whether present-day Arabs will confirm or deny it.

Mene/Selene
Dianna 2 other faces in ancient Greek myth.

Prosymne
Another face of Demeter in her underworld aspect, as the new moon

Hecate

Hecate, the new or dark moon, is generally taken to be the same as ta blending of Dianna the Moon and Proserpine. Hence her classical epithets Triceps and Triformis; referring to her other three faces and the three phases of the Selene first quarter Dianna Full and Mene last quarter. Eggs and onions, used to purify the house on the 30th of each month, were deposited for Hecate at three cross-roads. In the Julian calendar the old divisions of the lunar month were also retained... These were (a) the Kalendae, marking the first appearance of the new moon; (b) the Nonae, marking the first quarter; (c) the Idus, marking the full moon.

Govardhan Puja / Kali Puja

24 The Celtic Tree Moon of ELDER

Gaelic - Ruish - Nov 24 - Dec 23
A time of endings. Although the Elder can be damaged easily, it recovers quickly and springs back to life, corresponding to the approaching New Year. A good time for workings related to creativity and renewal. It is a time of beginnings and endings, births and deaths, and rejuvenation. Elder is also said to protect against demons and other negative entities. Use in magic connected to Faeries and other nature spirits.

24. Guru Nanak Jayanti
25. St Catherine
A Christian version of Nemesis, Goddess of the Wheel of Fate from which we get the custom of Catherin wheels. Burning wheels rolled down hills in the pagan fire festivals.

26. Day of Covenant – Baha'i

27 10:29 O MoonApogee:405900 km
30 19:30 Full O Moon
30 19:43 Pen. Lunar Eclipse

DECEMBER

1. The Festival Of Poseidon, the Greek god of the sea. Poseidon is also the god of rebirth

Crowley's "Greater Feast" A celebration to commemorate the death of Aleister Crowley on this day in 1947 e.v.

01 17:46 O Moon Ascending Node
03 11:22 O Moon North Dec:24.9° N

4.The Festival Of Bona Dea, Women Only Day - Roman fertility Goddess with secret rites in the house of prominent Roman magistrates. all representations of men and beasts were removed.

5. Faunalia (Roman) The festival of Faunus, the Roman god of wild nature and fertility. (A "Blokes World" day) Masculine balance of the above.

6 Earliest | Sunrise for the year – What would you like to start anew? Get up early write it on votive paper and offer it to the gentle dawn breeeze *Is this correct She"?*

8. Black Isis and the **'Immaculate Conception'** and annunciation 'in a dream', that the child to be born from her was the offspring of a God.
Anahita [Persian] Great Goddess of the Waters, Ardvi Sura Anahita the Heavenly Spring from which all waters on the earth flow down; A Cleansing Day

Feast of the Immaculate Conception of the Blessed **Virgin Mary**.
Bodhi Day (Rohatsu) - Buddhism
The Great She Bear Shamaness - the Grandmother of the indigenous North American

08 10:37 ◐ Last Quarter

9. The Optalia, the festival of Ops, the Roman Goddess of harvest.
The Virgin of Guadalupe [Mexican]- an old Aztec sky-goddess, who became the patron saint of all Mexico
The Unluckiest Day Of the Year – According to Grafton, the 16th century astrologer
9-16 Hannukah – Jewish

10. Liberty celebration in France. An actress is selected to personify the Goddess of Liberty. Being brought to Notre Dame, she is seated on the altar, and lights a large candle to signify that Liberty is the Light of the World.

13. The Sementivae, the second festival of Tellus, the Roman earth Goddess.

13 06:40 O Moon- ♀ Venus: 0.8° S
13 06:42 O Moon Perigee:361800 km
14 10:35 Geminid Shower: ZHR=120
14 21:03 O Moon Descending Node

15. The Second Festival Of Consus, the Roman god of good council

15 02:13 ☀ Total Solar Eclipse
15 02:17 ● New Moon
16 08:23 O Moon South Dec:24.9° S

17. The Saturnalia, First day of the seven-day festival of ♄ Saturn, the Roman god of agriculture. The most popular Roman festival. During this festival, business was suspended, the roles of master and slaves were reversed, moral restrictions were loosened, and gifts were exchanged. It was observed in memory of this Golden Age, at Saturn's temple on the Forum Romanum, below the Capitoline Hill.

17 14:28 O Moon- ♃ Jupiter: 3° N
17 15:25 O Moon- ♄ Saturn: 3.1° N

20. Festival for **Ammit/Al-Mawt** who was originally the ancestral spirit of the matriarchal culture in which the Feminine takes back what has been born of it. She was the underworld, the earth womb, as the perilous land of the dead through which the deceased must pass.

20 12:56 ☿ Mercury Superior Conj.

21. Vesta Capricorn was regarded as under the care of the goddess Vesta, and hence Vestae Sidus.
The Womb of Isis The adoration of the Mendesian Goat symbolised the Sun-God's resurrection in the House of the Goat (♑Capricorn) the Capricornian Goddess gives birth to the divine child of the next, year.
Amalthea [Greek] the nymph who fed Jupiter with goat's milk, one of whose horns broke off and was placed amongst the stars as Cornu Copiae, from which nectar and ambrosia were said to flow. Her principal star is Capella, the little goat. Therefore, Capricorn is the nurse of the youthful sun-god

Kore/Persephone The birth of the Divine Child, whether he bears the name of Horus, Osiris, Helios, Dionysus, or Aeon, was celebrated in the Koreion in Alexandria, the temple dedicated to Kore, on the day of the winter solstice.
Pryderi, [Celtic] son of Rhiannon, the virgin mother, is always born on the winter solstice.

20 12:56 ☿ Mercury Superior Conj.
21 20:02 Solstice

⊕ Major Sabbat LITHA

Summer Solstice - The longest day and the shortest night. A Time for Pagan revels and gatherings.

22 09:41 ◑ First Quarter
22 19:00 Ursid Shower: ZHR = 10
22 19:26 ♃ Jupiter ♄ Saturn: 0.1° N

♑ CAPRICORN

Cardinal Sign of ▽ Earth.

23. Celtic **"No Name day."** Shortest day of the year in the northern Hemisphere. This day was considered a whole month in the Celtic calendar 13 months plus The No Name Day. This was the day when the ☉sun did not come above the horizon in the northern part of the British Isles. The mythos was that the God of light Lugus, descended into the underworld and rose again on Yuletide day. On this day, Yule logs, representing his dying body, were lit to light the way of the god back to the upper realms. On the 25th he is resurrected an immortal. This was symbolised and celebrate by the decorated evergreen tree.
The Larentalia (Larentinalia), festival of Acca Larentia the Roman Goddess who gave the early Romans their land. The earth-Goddess, also called Sabine and Dea Tacita, the silent Goddess, a Roman Goddess of dead. On this day, offerings were brought to her in a mundus, an opened groove. She was honoured on this day at an altar in the Velabrium.

24 Celtic Tree Moon of BIRCH

Gaelic -Beth. Dec 24 - Jan 20
A time of rebirth and regeneration. As the Solstice passes, it is time to look towards the light once more. When a forested area burns, Birch is the first tree to grow back. Workings done in this month are good for adding momentum or for new endeavours. Birch is also associated with magick done for creativity and fertility, as well as healing and protection. Tie a red ribbon around the trunk of a Birch tree to ward off negative energy. Hang Birch twigs over a cradle to protect a newborn from harm. Use Birch bark as magickal parchment for spells.
Last Day of the Saturnalia Modraniht, or 'Night of the Mothers', was so called as the day preceding 'Child's Day' or 'Yule Day' long before the Anglo-Saxons were exposed to Christianity, thus proving its real character. Inscriptions are known from Roman times in Germany, Holland, and Britain, honour of

groups of female beings known generally as 'The Mothers'. Female deities of this kind seem to have been worshipped by both the Celts and the Germans, and they were evidently associated with fertility and with the protection of hearth and home.

25. Yule Eve Holiday. The Christian **Christmas Day**, At the end of the third century the Western Church adopted this pagan celebration (see below) day as the commemorative date of the birth of the Christos, and in time its decision was accepted also by the Eastern Church.
The Birthday Of Mithra, the Persian god of light and wisdom by his mother **Atargatis**.
Isis, the Virgo Caelestis, was believed to give birth to the Sun on the 25th of December.
Astarte festival celebrated in honour of the birth of the son of the Babylonian Queen of Heaven.
Myrrha [Greek] The mother of Adonis, was changed into a tree, and then gave birth to her divine son. From this we get the custom of the putting of the Yule Log into the fire on. As Zero-Ashta (Seed of Woman,) or Ignigena – (Born of Fire) he has to enter the fire on 'Mother night' that he may be born the next day out of it.
The Girl of the Yule Log Sometimes the log would be dragged in with a girl enthroned on it. In Scandinavia the ash symbolised the wood of the world-tree, Yggdrasil, & would be sprinkled with corn.
The Star Fairy The Christmas Tree, with its bright baubles and the star on top is a miniature version of the World Tree of our pagan ancestors, with its roots deep in the earth, the sun, moon and stars hung on its spreading branches, and the Pole Star at its topmost point. Sometimes the Star is replaced by a Goddess, ruling over the World.
Dionysus/Bacchus was transformed into a tree to avoid murder by his jealous stepmother Hera. The Titans uprooted him and burnt him but he was resurrected. During the Saturnalia, a decorated pine tree was hung with little masks of Dionysus/ Bacchus to commemorate this.
Nullog Day in Ancient Irish, meaning 'New Belly' 'being born anew'. They crawled through holes in the logs representing passing issuing through the womb to a new life.
26. SE Asia, partial NW Australia
Boxing Day – Day for giving gifts to the less fortunate and those that depend on you
Yule Tide Day - Day One Of the Twelve Days -Yule is related to Norse word 'Iul,' meaning 'Wheel' and 'Light', and Saxon word for 'Sun'. Ancient Egyptians at the Winter Solstice used a palm branch containing twelve leaves or shoots to symbolize the 'completion of the year'.
Sweetie Scone Day [Scotland] Scones and "Currant Loaf" were baked from the rich, sweet ingredients in the boxes given to the beneficiaries who could not afford the luxury of dried fruit and spices Neighbours would share ingredients and then share the sweets.

25 02:32 ○ Moon Apogee: 405000 km
Zarathosht Diso Death of Prophet Zarathushtra – Zoroastrian
26 Dec - Jan 1 **Kwanzaa** – Interfaith.
27. **Yule Eve** Spiritual rebirth for old souls **Nut's Birthing Day** After the twelfth month of each year and before the first day of the ensuing year, the Egyptians allowed five days to permit Nut to give birth to all her children.
Festival for The Horae, controllers of the wheel of time, who presided over all changes of time and watched over the works of men. They were goddesses of order in nature represented as delicate, joyous, lightly moving beings adorned with flowers and fruits.
29. **The Egyptian remembrance of The Hours** The Egyptians were the first to divide the day into 24 hours; there were twelve hours of the day and twelve to the night. Each was allocated a goddess standing in a boat, The 'Lady of the Boat' changed every hour.
29 01:03 ○ Moon Ascending Node
30. On this day **Hathor gives birth to the sun Ra**, in the form of the Scarab beetle,
Isis birthday The Egyptian year consisted of twelve months of 30 days each making only 360 days: thus five intermediary days, called 'the thirteenth month', were added to make the year a complete 365. Isis, governed the fourth intercalary day, which was celebrated as her birthday.
30 13:28 Full ○ Moon
30 17:53 ○ Moon North Dec:24.9° N
31. **New Year's Eve**
Nephthys The fifth intercalary day was celebrated as the birthday of Nephthys,
Sekhmet Goddess of Time: If you get a vision of Sekhmet on this day will be fortunate.
Hestia/Vesta is the Genius of the home-fire, and it is traditional on this day to bless the house by making the Pentacle in the four corners of each room. Ivy is hung on the outer doors to protect the house against evil through the coming year.
Ancient Graeco-Egyptian New Years Eve Feast Set a luxurious table with exotic articles of food, and with goblets of new wine, for a fruitful New Year. The Egyptian year began at a different time from ours, but this is as near as possible the way in which Hogmanay is still observed on the last day of the last month of the year in Scotland.
Hogmanay is New Year's Night preceding the Hagmena, or Holy Month on which a table is spread, with buns and other dainties, oatcakes, cheese and strong drink is essential. For the Irish anything which happened on New Year's Eve and Day might divinity of the future, and the nearer to the midnight hour when the year actually began, the more significant.
Entering The Age of Cailleach Bheara corresponds to the maturity of humanity. This is an era of reawakened psychic and artistic sensitivity, of renewed magical powers and of growing religious knowledge.

Join us on line for times and sidereal astrological potential for each day for your magickal workings

FUNNY PHOTOS

ENHANCING RITUALS WITH CRYSTALS

by Ronnie Lee Dearlove

Crystals are magical gifts from Mother Earth, each as individual as their keeper. Their structures, forms and properties are as varied as the ways they can be of assistance to us, in essences, grids, altar decoration, healing and rituals. My connection with spirit and crystals has developed over the last twenty years. I am continually amazed by the beauty and energy of crystals and their ability to assist my development on a daily basis. I prefer to utilise crystals that have been gifted by Mother Earth in an ethical and gentle way so as to minimise the impact my practices have on her. This issue I will focus on ways to use crystals to enhance the festival of *Beltane*. The focus of Beltane is on:

- fertility and passion
- improvement of a career, financial or business matters
- increasing commitment in love and inspiring passion
- creative inspiration
- improving health and increasing energy levels
- abundance
- generosity
- optimism
- self-confidence
- conceiving

Crystals come in many, different colours and forms. Colours associated with the festival of Beltane are:

- **Green** - abundance, growth, fertility
- **Red** - strength, vitality, passion, vibrancy
- **Silver** - cleansing, dispersing negative energy
- **Pearl** - balances emotions, symbol of fertility, passion.

There are an endless array of beautiful crystals to choose from. I have selected crystals this issue that are easily sourced and affordable and correspond with the colours that represent Beltane. Some crystals that you may wish to connect with during Beltane to activate and enhance the power and connection of your rituals are:

- **Ruby** - *Root Chakra*, security and self-esteem, enhances confidence, power, passion, friendship.
- **Carnelian** - *Sacral Chakra* - brings love of life, overcomes negative conditioning, increases trust in your judgement and perceptions, calms anger, passion.
- **Citrine** - *Solar Plexus Chakra* - brings abundance, activates creativity, manifests and attracts wealth, prosperity and success, absorbs/transmutes/dissipates negative energy, energizes every level of life, is an aura protector. It also activates the Crown Chakra and opens the intuition. Cleanses and balances and aligns the subtle bodies.
- **Rose Quartz** - *Heart Chakra* - for unconditional love, self-love and infinite peace.
- **Emerald** - *Heart Chakra* - inspiration and patience, eliminates negativity, to bring forth positive action and encourage group understanding.
- **Sapphire** - *Throat Chakra* - (Blue) wisdom, to focus the mind, and release unwanted thoughts and intentions, can restore balance within the body.
- **Herkimer Diamond** - *Third Eye Chakra* - aids psychic vision and dream/meditation recall.
- **Amethyst** - *Throat & Crown Chakras* - balances and connects physical, mental and emotional bodies, cleanses the aura, and transmutes negative energy, also brings restful sleep, a shift in consciousness, faithfulness in love, and freedom from jealousy.

Crystals in Ritual

Crystals may be used to activate the energies you are aligning with and to enhance your rituals. Rituals are very personal and I encourage you to adapt and enhance your rituals using your intuition to select your crystals. Another use for crystals is griding your sacred space before you cast circle. The crystals you choose to grid your sacred space will vary according to the ritual you wish to perform. You may wish to choose from the list above, or you may decide to grid with Clear Quartz which is a powerful crystal for amplifying the energy of the ritual you are performing and for bringing clarity. There are many different ways to lay a crystal grid, some more complex than others. A basic way to grid your sacred space is to place your crystal of choice in each corner of the room you are using, or perhaps place clear quartz crystals in a circle where you wish to cast circle or around your altar. When using crystals there are no rules, simply connect with your intuition and let your creative energies flow freely.

Love and Blessings)O(Ronnie Lee

Ronnie Lee is a serene soul whose wisdom is subtle yet powerful. Her natural instinct and intuitive talents are strong and she shows warmth and love in her connection with you. Ronnie lee is a wise woman who has much to share and lives life in a search for all that is good and honest, she radiates compassion and love and has many insights to share. Connecting you through your heart, the cosmic heart and the earth's heart. Using crystals, sacred geometry, grids, ritual, and the elements to intuitively balance your chakras, clear your aura, reveal your soul brilliance. Ronnie Lee is a Crystal Magickal Practitioner, Essence of Angels Teacher, and Crystal Light Healing Teacher. Based on the Sunshine Coast. Circle of Soul Brilliance

www.csgbribieisland.wixsite.com/csgbi   www.facebook/csgbi Email: csgbi@mail.com

LOVE INVOCATION

You will need:
- 4 x Rose Quartz Crystals
- 1 x Large Amethyst Crystal
- 5 x Pink Candles
- Silk Altar Cloth
- Any other symbols, herbs, oils and tools that you are drawn to use.

Cast circle. Layout your crystals and candles - place one rose quartz crystal and one pink candle in each of the four directions on your altar (North, West, South and East) welcoming the element, spirits, gods and goddess' you wish to invoke for each direction as you light each candle. Place the amethyst crystal and one candle in the centre of the altar.

Sitting in front of your altar, hold each crystal in your hands, close your eyes as you connect to the energy of the crystal and focus on your intent for this ritual. Feel the energy flow from the crystal into your hands, through your body to your heart. Feel your heart open up to the energy of love, feel the love expand your heart, Focus on expanding the love out from your heart to the Heart of the Earth. Feel the love flow freely between your heart and the Earth's Heart and extend the flow of love up to the Heart of the Cosmos. Connect the energy flow of love to the cosmic heart to your heart through to the Earth's heart and up again in the infinity symbol. Expand this beautiful loving energy to encompass your home, your relationships, your lifestyle, your world. Focus on welcoming LOVE into your heart, and your life. Sit in this energy for as long as you are compelled to do so.

When you feel you are ready to close the ritual state "I call love into my life" as you blow out each candle. Close circle. Leave the crystals on the altar for as long as you wish. Or you may wish to place them around your bed or carry them with you for a period of time. This is a ritual to bring love into your life, it is not meant to impose on the free will of another person.

You may wish to select other crystals to suit your intent for the ritual and this is perfect for you at this time. Use your intuition and connect with the crystal that resonates with you. You may adapt this ritual to incorporate your other tools and invocations as you desire.

CUDDLE THERAPY

When I separated from my long term partner, I soon realised how important touch was to me. Yes, I had taken it for granted all those years. It was something I didn't even realise was supporting me and nourishing me, until it was gone. It became a real struggle for me to get sufficient touch and human connection in my life. Yet I didn't want to be in a relationship with anyone, as I was still processing my separation.

Then my Facebook feed coughed up an interesting event. There was a Cuddle Club being run on the other side of town by a woman called Deborah Toussaint, who, as part of her healing and spiritual practice offered cuddle therapy. So I went along, and was held and cuddled for nearly two hours, in a small and intimate group.

I felt great, and was high for days. But now I had a problem. Cuddle Club was on the other side of town, and work commitments meant I couldn't get there except during holiday time. So I decided I would have to make my own Cuddle Club. I enrolled in the online Diploma of Cuddle Therapy with Cuddle Therapy Australia, and now a fully qualified professional cuddler, I have begun to hold a regular cuddle pod in my home at Mount Nebo, outside Brisbane, and have even appeared on the Fitzy and Wippa radio show talking about cuddle therapy.

The physical benefits of a cuddle are well documented scientifically. A sustained cuddle prompts the body to release Oxytocin, one of the feel good chemicals of the brain, sometimes called the "cuddle hormone", which fosters a sense of connection and bonding with others. Touch can also reduce heart rate, lower blood pressure, reduce feelings of anxiety and depression, and stimulate feelings of compassion.

However the type of touch is very important. We have different types of touch receptors in the skin. It is the Merkel cells in the very base of the skin that appear to be most important in the release of oxytocin and combatting stress. These cells respond to pressure, such as a firm but gentle holding. This is the type of touch that is most often employed in cuddle therapy. Other types of touch, such as light stroking, activate different receptor cells. Such touch may be perceived as sensuous with the right person in the right situation, but otherwise may be perceived as creepy. Likewise squeezing can often be perceived as aggressive, or as an attempt to control. Both these types of touches are avoided in cuddle therapy.

The intention behind the touch is very important as well. Research has shown that people are surprisingly good at picking up the emotion being communicated by even a short touch. Research by Dacher Keltner found people were right more than 50% of the time when asked to identify emotions such as compassion, anger, gratitude, love and fear, just by someone's touch. So a clear compassionate intention behind the therapeutic cuddle is also important, as this is communicated directly to the person being touched.

As people get older, especially those without a long term relationship, they tend to suffer even more from lack of touch - and the consequent elevation of depression, anxiety, and cardiovascular problems. One response to this need is the professional cuddle therapist, who can offer a paid service to people needing compassionate touch, but who can't otherwise access it due to their circumstances.

However one on one cuddle therapy sessions may be too expensive for many people, which is why I have chosen to run a group session I call the cuddle pod. In this way people can have all the benefits of touch, in a safe and facilitated environment, at a much reduced cost. After demonstrating non sexual touch, and empowering people to speak out if they find something uncomfortable, we move through a range of different cuddle postures, with different partners and as a group. These could involve hand holding, sitting back to back, sitting side by side with legs crossed, holding from behind, holding someone's head in your lap, spooning, as well as the standard hug we are all familiar with.

There are many other things that could be said about the healing power of touch and its importance in our lives, and how we may engage with each other in a more healthy way. Not least of which is how to break down the patriarchal attitudes that have caused so much distress through unwanted and inappropriate sexualised touch. One thing I am hoping to do as a male cuddle therapist is to help men unlink sexuality and touch, learn to give and receive compassionate touch with other men, and to be sensitive to and respectful of everyone's bodily sovereignty.

Rob Reeves is a musician and guitar teacher, a professional palmist and tarot card reader, and cuddle therapist. He is the director of studies at Llan Mor Gwen, which teaches magic, mysticism and spirituality through encountering Celtic Deities and folklore. He may be contacted at robscuddles@gmail.com

SEKHEM: EGYPTIAN LIVING LIGHT

What is Sekhem? Sekhem is an ancient Egyptian form of *healing*. References to it have been discovered in the Egyptian Book of the Dead and in ancient papyri. A gift to the world from the Goddess Sekhmet, the mother of all healing goddesses. Sekhmet has her healing and protective aspects. While many only remember her as the ferocious consort of the Sun god Ra, she is also a master of the art of medicine as she provides the cure to various ailments.

Sekhem Energy Healing is a non-invasive ancient Egyptian energy healing modality that is channelled through the hands, in a similar manner to Reiki, to help realign, release and shift the blocked / stagnant layers of energy around the body.

We have the opportunity to bring **The World's Leading Sekhem Practitioner** to Australia for the first time, late next year after international borders open again (Nov 2021).

Please register your interest :-
✆ 0402 793 604 / magickmagazine1@gmail.com

Sekhem Master Ruby T. Ong from Hong Kong describes her foundation level class in her own words:

Living Light Energy is an advanced energy healing system. Like Reiki, it is a channelled energy with a higher vibrational level. Both Reiki and Seichim are encompassed within the greater healing power of *Living Light Energy* for it is considered to be the origin of all hands-on healing systems, as it was taught in the very early temples of ancient Egypt, Lemuria and Atlantis.

Living Light Energy works on all the physical, mental, emotional and subtle spiritual bodies at the same time. There is completeness to *Living Light Energy* that goes way beyond other systems. It works at the soul level. Because of its power, thought forms and intention activate it consciously. Also the energy can be directed, its intensity controlled and varied at will.

Learn this subtle yet powerful energy where focus is on empowering the individual to develop their own path, to promote oneness and self-healing, healing of others and healing any other problem in one's life.

Learn to master the flow of energy. This is a powerful ancient Egyptian vibrational healing modality. Topics include: sensing energy, understanding illness and healing, cleansing the auric field, channeling, moving and directing the energy flow, creating a sacred space and a safe environment, creating forgiveness, techniques of self healing and protection. Activities include meditation, interactive discussion and experiential hands-on healing techniques.

Ruby T. Ong is an experienced healer and caring teacher who takes pride in empowering the individual to maximize their own potential. She believes that, with self-empowerment, people will be more aware that they have a response-ability to live their life with their vision of faith. She is also well trained in different levels of Pranic Healing. Her personal public relations consultancy M V Reach Communications is a major organizer of holistic events in Hong Kong.

HELP PAGANISM TO BECOME A RECOGNISED DENOMINATION IN AUSTRALIA

I am a "Religious" Pagan marriage celebrant.
I am *the "last" legal religious Pagan celebrant* in Australia.

PLEASE SIGN OUR PETITION HERE:
https://www.change.org/p/attorney-general-s-department-allow-paganism-to-become-a-recognised-denomination-in-australia

Our government has deemed all celebrants, civil, unless they are from a registered religion, which I am. However, they will not allow any other celebrants to become "religious Pagan" unless Paganism becomes a registered denomination. Sadly, even though there are many registered Pagan churches and groups ready to band together to become a denomination, the Attorney General's Department is not allowing our application for an umbrella Pagan religious denomination to go through. Thirty-six Pagan religious organisations have banded together to do this. Yet, the Australian Attorney-General's Department's reason for the denial is because "They" don't consider Paganism to be an organised religion.

So, an arbitrary decision has been made, a judgment call, by someone with opposing religious views, hidden behind a desk somewhere, to limit your religious freedom. This decision affects every Australian and Pagan, all around the world. You have to tell them that is not acceptable. Say "NO" loudly and clearly. Otherwise, in the near future we may not be able to hold beautiful ceremonies like this, legally, any more   - https://youtu.be/GsQALE_Te1I   and we will have **moved back one step closer to the dark ages** and a **return to the witch hunts.**

STAND UP & SAY "**NO**" TO THAT!!!!

It would be wonderful if we all could show support for religious freedom, of a group that has no dogma, is empowering, honours the individual, follows a nature based belief system, that is highly ethical, has no extremist history and that hurts no one. In fact, during the recent 'Royal Commission into Victimisation by Religious Organisations' there were "zero" complaints lodged against any Pagan group or organisation. However, what we really do, is hold beautiful and meaningful ceremonies like the handfasting in this Youtube clip.

Please show your support for what Australia could loose if Pagan Religious celebrants become extinct with my demise. **Please demand that your religious freedoms be upheld by signing this petition.**

Thank You & Every Bright Blessing to you,
Reverend. Dr S. D'Montford (D.D. HPs)

http://www.shedmontford.com/magickal-weddings.html

BOOKS BY SHÉ D'MONTFORD

DEMONOLOGY — $20
The belief in demons is not universal – Follow the history of the creation of demons to discover what they really are

IBOGAINE — $20
An ancient cure for addiction in one treatment without withdrawals

GOETIA — $20
A modern translation of this text on how to work with the Goeting beings without the overlay of Christian culture demonisation

SCRYING: THE ART OF SEEING THE FUTURE WITH OMENS & DIVINATION — $25
Tea Leaf Reading, Runes, Oghams, Gematria, Dreams, Clouds, Fire, Chinese Ink and more

SEVEN PSYCHIC SECRETS — $25
BEST SELLER - Seeing Auras, Moving & Feeling Energy, Psychometry, Remote Viewing, Working With Spirit, Healing & Remote healing

QUICK SPELLS — $10
For the seven most wished for things

THE INNER GODDESS WORKOUT — $29
40 Goddesses & how to work with them - Illustrations by Wanda Shipton

THE CANCER ANSWER — $10
Legitimate, Approved effective cure, that is that has been available since 1950 but that the medical industry will not tell you about. WHY?

WHO'S AFRAID OF THE BIG BAD WITCH? — $29
Exploding the most common Lies about the Craft of the Wise

WOMEN WHO MARRY ANGELS: — $25
Collected Works of Ida Craddock

SPIRIT SHOTS — $29
200 photos of ghosts and spirits. What is death & how to work with the spirit realm.

PENDULUM DOWSING: — $10
Discover the Secrets of Dowsing

IMPROVE PHYSICAL AND SPIRITUAL VISION — $10
Physical and spiritual exercises to improve your vision

THE MAGIC STORY — $10
The Secret of Success - Written in 1700s, Rewritten in 1901. Reprinted today, More relevant than ever

MAGICK 8: FOR THOSE WHO BELIEVE — $12.95
Back Issue

AVAILABLE FROM ALL GOOD BOOK STORES - Distributed through Ingram Spark

THE WITCHES BALL 2019

PHOTO CREDITS Ken Wills

Amy Hanson hosted another magickal evening at The Tivoli. The venue is perfect, old and haunted, with many reporting seeing ghosts in the bathrooms after imbibing a substantial amount of alcohol. There were over 250 witches in amazing costumes, enchanting performances, spellbinding stalls, witchin' readers, a "Shake Your Fat" dance & a true sense of community. It was a ritual event that binds all as one. Amy delivered this service to the South East Qld Pagan community despite financial difficulties, separating from her partner and the death of her mother. However, the Covind19 scare has forced her to cancel her 2020 event. Let's hope it will be rescheduled to a future date. -

We love you Amy. Your service to the community is deeply appreciated!!!

Magick Magazine No. 10

MAGICKAL CLASSIFIDES

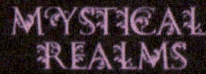

A place where magical energies come together, entwining the uniqueness of each individual's own spiritual path to proudly celebrate who we are. You will fit in at Mystic Realms Witchcraft

• Gatherings • Workshops • Esbat
• Sabbats • Unique and needful things for the craft of the wise

Go to www.mysticalrealmswitchcraft.com for upcoming events and other useful stuff.
Remember to like us on Facebook

REMEMBER
Go to our facebook page & send us a message about your free/non-profit magickal events so that we can list it here & tell everyone in the community !
https://www.facebook.com/MagickMagazine/

Astrovisuals
Supplying Astronomical Visual Materials including Calendars, Apps, Star & Moon maps & novelties. Manufactured in Australia.
mail@astrovisuals.com.au
https://www.astrovisuals.com/
0431 193 396

TAKE A SELFIE
reading Magick Magazine. Make the photo memorable or in an amazing location. Then send it to us for a chance to win great prizes & you might even see yourself in the pages of Magick too!

GOLD COAST WITCHES' BREW
A friendly, informal coffee morning for those interested in Witchcraft, Wicca, Druidry or any other form of Paganism and/or Earth Based Spirituality.

ALL WELCOME!

WHEN: Last Monday of each month from 10.30am to approx 12.30pm
WHERE: Cafe Campanile, Robina Town Centre, Gold Coast, Queensland.
Want more details?
Phone: 0402066330 or
Email: morganna13@hotmail.com

Woman's Spiritual Wiccan Coven of Gold Coast
Live life magically and spiritually attuned with nature. Fortnightly to Monthly Meet Ups. To find out more go to
www.meetup.com/WiccanCoven

REMEMBER: Go to our facebook page & send us a message about your free/non-profit magickal events so that we can list it here & tell everyone in the community !

REMEMBER
CHECK OUR PAGES
for more magickal competitions and giveaways
from our advertisers, events and other cool stuff
www.magick.org.au
Facebook
https://www.facebook.com/MagickMagazine/
Group
https://www.facebook.com/groups/magickmagazine/

Professional Psychic Reading Service is located in Gold Coast, Australia. We helped change the lives of hundreds of satisfied customers from around the world through psychic readings.
www.barbspsychicreadings.com

Barb's Psychic Readings
0450 593 196

Lucy Cavendish & Shé D'Montford are pictured here with Sarah-Fay at Earth Spirit in Orange

EARTH SPIRIT IN ORANGE HAS MOVED

Our lovely Sarah says: "My new address is:

Shop 3/ 222 Anson St Orange NSW

We have all of our regular merchandise at the new shop. There are online events coming up, like workshops, courses & meditations that I am doing & our online store is still here for you too. We are still planning our Al Hallows Eve ball too
!! CHECK IT OUT !!

https://www.facebook.com/events/530501044475329

HOW TO CONTROL PEOPLE

LAO TZU'S ADVICE TO HIS EMPEROR ABOUT HOW TO CONTROL PEOPLE WITHOUT RIOT OR WARFARE

(Create a situation whereby) "The people take death seriously and do not travel far.

Though they have boats and carriages, no one uses them. Though they have armor and weapons, only for display. Men forget the art of reading & writing. Their food is plain paupers food but plentiful, their clothes fine but look like paupers clothes, they have a feeling of security at home & are just happy to not be bothered.

Though they live within sight of their neighbours & crowing cocks & barking dogs are heard across the way, they never bother to go there.

Then they leave each other in peace while they grow old and die and are never trouble to their Emperor. "

Tao Te Ching - Lao Tzu - chapter 80

SYMBOLS & THEIR MEANINGS

Scrying In All Its Many Forms

I've just been going through my photos from the last couple of weeks thinking about what I can write about for this article and came across a whole lot of different pics from readings and the symbols I have taken. Not just in the teacup, but from the Crystal Ball and cloud formations and even from paint peeling from a step and from a wall, the meanings are universal.

When you are open, you will get messages in all different forms.

Teacup - a nurse and needle. The nurse looks like she is wearing an old fashion cap like the nuns use to wear. The lady I was reading for had healing of old wounds, or completion of a project.

A surprise is looming for you that will create one of the most wonderful moments of your life. This is a message of glorious accomplishments that will set the standards for years to come.

I see Dragon's all the time and it may be because I was born in the Year of the Dragon. I do feel the Dragon's protection.

Phoenix – that is on our steps at home created by the wear and tear and paint peeling. Meaning - Rebirth, longevity triumph, healing, rising above everything.

down to the bay after and in the clouds, I could see a dog and a puppy beside her. Charlotte daughter Lily had died before her from a tick many years ago and she was the runt of the litter and always looked like a puppy. So, I felt she had been met by her daughter. The photo didn't really pick it up well.

Another reading I did last Thursday or Friday as a collect for all using the Witchypoo Brew "Love" tea blend on my live show , I held up the cup for everyone to see and most could see very clearly a symbol of Australia and a horse with a rider. The horse with a rider is money coming in. On Monday the

-Scooby-   -Australia-   -Phoenix-   -Nurse-   -Dragon-

Polio and she had been to young to be vaccinated against it or her mum hadn't been vaccinated. It was also when the Covid19 Virus had just started to cause places to shut down. I thought it may have something to do with that too.

Clouds – dragon (extract from my book) New beginnings, beware of enemies, courage, strength and fortitude. The Dragon is victorious in any situation and serves as a powerful guide and guardian in business, work and family. Victory comes in emotional triumph and

Scooby – again from paint peeling on a wall. Reminded me of a reading I had done not so long ago at MBS at Brisbane Convention Centre. The lady I was reading for had lost her Doberman 3 weeks before and his name was Scooby, the lady next to her picked it up in her cup. I was live on Facebook when I was doing that reading in front of about 80 people.

On Friday 13th March I had to get my beautiful girl Charlotte put down. She was 16 years old Maltese and had suffered a stroke and probably had a form of breast cancer. I went

government announced that it would be giving out a stimulus package to help people affected by the virus. Even though I had to shut down my business until whenever, I was never worried. I just had faith that all would be fine. Now I have time to write another book or two and set up my workshops online. I'm excited. I know there are good time ahead.

Magical blessings to you all. Your angels are watching over you.

Love Kate.

Kate Denning is a modern day Mystic, talented Clairvoyant, and Spiritual Teacher/Mentor. Kate is highly skilled in the ancient art of Tea Leaf Reading, as well as Palmistry and Crystal Ball Reading. Kate offers one on one readings, psychic parties, workshops, and live talks.
FB: The Rendezvous Tea Room
Or The Spiritual Realm with Kate Denning
787 Stanley Street Woolloongabba Qld 4102
The A – Z of Tea Leaf Reading by Kate Denning RR $20
www.thespiritualrealm.com.au

Our next Magick Magazine will be issue eleven

The 10 Sepheroth
of the Kabhallah

The Dark Side:
When things go wrong in 'Spiritual Groups'

The mystic art of Alex Gray
& his new **ENTHEON** temple space project

Learn the Hieroglyphic Alphabet

Plus
- Spells,
- Herbs,
- Events
- Reviews,
- The Weekly Seer
- Erotic Pagan Fiction
- The Witches' Almanac
- & much, much, more!

And a few surprises too!!!

WINDSONG
The Real Mother of
Mother, I Feel You Under My Feet

Image - Sanctuum Vite by The Wayfarer - Rhadé Shojh 2020

Next issue will be out soon… Apologies that this magazine is late - This has been a crazy year for me, our contributors, our advertisers… and for you too! We all appreciate your patience. I have an absolute commitment to make sure that our subscribers get all of the number of issues that they have paid for. We are soldering on into the future and are exploring other options like drop shipping for subscriptions rather than direct handling of magazines for post which has been hard for us to organise with those people who have been helping us with our order fulfilment.

Thank you for you understanding during these troubled times - Stay Safe.
In perfect love and perfect trust whilst wishing you every blessing

Your Editor
Shé D'Montford

Order Now:
www.magick.org.au

Ways You Can Connect With Your Guides

Connecting with our guides is a magickal connection that will empower you and help you with your own journey . It will give you an inner knowing that you are on the right path in your life, and you will also feel that no matter what, you are never alone. There are many ways to connect with your guides, I am going to go through some of the ways that work for me. You may have your own ways that work for you that are different, there are no right or wrong ways to connect in with these energies, whatever works for you is what you should use. This will give you a power and strength that comes from having a Divine energy guiding you, and this feels amazing.

If you cannot connect with your guides try some of these methods until you find the one that works for you. It won't happen overnight, it will take time and some deep inner work from you, but the results when you get the connection are well worth the efforts. They may be Angels, Goddesses, Gods, Elementals , loved ones that have passed, etc, but whoever they may be , they are there to guide you on this rollercoaster called life.

Firstly before I connect I will always do a meditation to open my chakras from the Base Chakra up to the Crown Chakra. This means you will be open to receive messages and will have more chance to connect in to these Divine energies. Please before you do this make sure you protect yourself with a white or gold circle of light around you as you are opening yourself up to other energies. Also once you have finished any work you do with your chakras open, please go through them starting from the Crown chakra and going down and close your chakras and ground yourself again. So once your Chakras are open to receive, you will be ready to connect to your guides.

The first way that I connected with my guides was through my dreams, so pay attention to anyone trying to contact you through your dreams, as it could be guides, spirit animals , loved ones etc.

The next method that worked for me was to put myself into a trance like state through meditation, and then ask a question with a pen and paper at the ready. This is called Automatic Writing. Then you just write whatever comes into your head without even thinking about it. Read it back when you are finished and see if it helps with your question. I get lots of guidance through automatic writing and it has also worked when doing readings for other people.

Sarah connecting with her spirit guides

Meditation is a great way to connect. Just ask your guides to come in and give you guidance in regards to a certain situation , and then see what happens. My messages from my guides always come from my right hand side , and I have one guide that is my main guide who I work with all the time, but there are also 2 others and guides that come and go according to what help I may need at the time. The messages seem to come down into my right hand ear. You may also see images and pictures, this is also messages for you. Messages from your left hand side are usually family who have passed.

Sitting in nature is a beautiful place to connect with your guides as well. Pick a quiet place that you feel comfortable in and again go into a meditative trance like state, ask the question in your head, and sit and listen.

But if you get that connection and your guides can see you want their help, you will get guidance from them quite often the more you ask for it.

Another way they can connect is for you to see numbers all the time, the same numbers . For me it is always the number 3 as it is my Numerology number and a very spiritual number as well. And I know they are trying to get my attention if I see 3, or 333 or even 111 as this adds up to 3.

So I hope you try some of these methods to connect and even try some others of your own and see how you go. It is a very special magickal connection that will empower you and help you through your life..

Magick and Blessings

Sarah-Fay

MAGICK MAGAZINE'S
ONLINE COURSE IN MAGICK

EVERYONE CAN PERFORM MAGICK. To a lesser extent we do it every day. Our WILL shapes our world. We make sure that we get the things we like & influence people to see things our way. But we can learn to do so much more. You can learn to do Magick far more effectively. We can get results in a scientifically repeatable way.

SHÉ D'MONTFORD WILL SHOW YOU HOW.

Learn esoteric skills from **AURA SEEING** to **THE ZIGI**. Learn magickal methods from **INDIGENOUS MAGICK** of the Australia Aborigines through to the **HIGH MAGICK** of the elite ceremonial magickians. From **BASIC CANDLE** & **SIGAL MAGICK** through to **TIME TRAVEL & TRANSCENDENCE**.

THESE ARE TESTED METHODS THAT WORK!

Shé has a deep, extensive curriculum that she has taught around the world since 1990. Shé teaches magick without the nonsense. Magick, when you do it right, is not that hard. Learning the right way from a good teacher is the necessary thing. View the curriculum online www.shedmontford.com/curriculum.html Now, Shé D'Montford's classes are moving into the digital age to make all the Magick available to you in a practical & easy to learn package. These classes will be live & pre-recorded, online courses, with the ability to interact directly with Shé D'Montford & ask her questions.

Shé D'Montford has been traveling around the world to make herself available to teach empowering magick to eager students in person. Now, with the aid of digital technology, Shé can be available to all sincere seekers, anywhere in the world, all the time, Packages will bundle together units that are usually about $95 each, for the low price of only $25 per month. YOU can save thousands & YOU can have personal tuition no matter where in the world YOU live, whenever it is convenient for YOU to learn.

Sign up for to our exclusive subscribers group, for as little as $25 per month & enjoy having full access to all that you can possibly learn or you can purchase specific packages. There is a recommended order to the lessons to help you progress. Join up for your no risk beginners course today. There is a 30-day money back guarantee if you are not happy & you can unsubscribe at any time.

GO TO www.magick.org.au & BEGIN A MAGICKAL LIFE TODAY

BONUS:
Every subscriber receives Magick Magazine for free for the duration of their subscription to their magickal tuition.

www.ingramcontent.com/pod-product-compliance
Lightning Source LLC
Chambersburg PA
CBHW080900010526
44118CB00015B/2219